ZEN GUIDE

Zen Guide

Where to Meditate in Japan

by Martin Roth
and John Stevens

New York · WEATHERHILL · *Tokyo*

First edition, 1985
Second printing, 1991

Published by Weatherhill, Inc., New York, with editorial offices at
Tanko-Weatherhill, Inc., 8-3 Nibancho, Chiyoda-ku, Tokyo 102, Japan.
Protected by copyright under terms of the International Copyright Union;
all rights reserved. Printed and first published in Japan.

Library of Congress Cataloging in Publication Data: Roth, Martin. / Zen
guide. / Bibliography: p.   / Includes index. / 1. Temples, Zen—Japan—
Guide–books. / 2. Meditation (Zen Buddhism) / I. Stevens, John, /
1947–   . / II. Title. / BQ 6352.R67   1985 / 294.3′927′0952 / 85–7155 /
ISBN 0–8348–0202–3

Contents

Other Areas   54

Full-Time Training and Ordination   68

PART TWO: RELATED ACTIVITIES

Temple Accommodations   79

Food for Practice   93

Preface

This book serves three types of seekers: newcomers who want to actually experience basic Buddhism; long-time meditators who need information on advanced training; and those who plan to devote themselves exclusively to Buddhism, either as ordained monks or nuns or as full-time lay students. For the sympathetic tourist as well there are sections on temples that accommodate guests overnight (*shukubō*), restaurants offering Buddhist vegetarian fare (*shōjin ryōri*), and Buddhist temple pilgrimages, popular routes for sightseeing as well as religious devotion. Finally, there is a note on Buddhist academic institutions for scholars.

While the majority of places mentioned here are associated with Zen, the best-known form of Japanese Buddhism and the most receptive to foreign students, the listings include many excellent training centers affiliated with other traditions. Some worthwhile centers and a few of the finest teachers have been omitted at their request; once contacts have been established, however, the names of those places will eventually become known and proper introductions can be arranged.

When using this guide keep firmly in mind these three pearls of Buddhist wisdom: "All things are impermanent," "All things are imperfect," and "Everything depends." Conditions continually change: group leaders transfer, resign, retire, or die; temple doors suddenly close to outsiders; organizations radically alter their orientation overnight. Always confirm the current status of any place you plan to visit. Every center has disadvantages. None of the listings has our unreserved recommendation, and you will never find the perfect place. Everyone's needs differ. The suitability of a training center for any given practitioner depends on a host of inner and outer variables. Thus, we cannot grade or rank the listings.

It is impossible to mention all the kind people who freely gave of their time and knowledge to help in the preparation of this book. In particular, we would like to thank Jose Caldeira, Griff Faulk, Rev. Masao Ichishima, Gudō Wafū Nishijima, Steve Powell, Ian Reader, Ann Sargent, Priscilla Storandt, Tom Wright, and the staff of John Weatherhill. Thanks also to Junko Kawasaki for making so many phone calls.

Portions of this book appeared, in very different form, in the *Asahi Evening News, East-West Journal,* and the *Mainichi Daily News.*

As much as we would like to guide our readers, trouble free, along the Path, we can do no more than point the way. The intricacies of Buddhist practice can never be adequately explained with words or pictures: "If you want to know if the water is hot or cold, you must taste it yourself."

Martin Roth
John Stevens

Introduction

THE WAY OF BUDDHA   Some 2,500 years ago in the kingdom of Shakya, located in what is now southern Nepal, the handsome young prince Siddhartha was in torment, despite his incomparably comfortable circumstances. Siddhartha used only the sweetest smelling incense and wore nothing but the finest, most costly cloth; day and night a canopy shielded him from heat, cold, wind, and dust; he had three magnificent residences, one each for summer, winter, and the rainy season; the choicest delicacies graced his table; servants and court maidens were continually on hand to cater to his every need; he enjoyed perfect health, and his lovely wife and infant son were the envy of all.

Yet the prince was dissatisfied. He had observed, one day, insects being swallowed by birds and those birds in turn being devoured by hawks, and ever since the suffering and distress of other beings sorely troubled him. Later, on a brief trip outside the palace walls, Siddhartha caught a glimpse of the fate that awaits all humans. At the age of twenty-nine, the thought of old age, disease, and death filled Siddhartha with dread and drained him of his vigor.

"My heart will never be at rest until I fathom the true nature of this world," he despaired. "I must flee this place and look for the answers to my questions." Late that night, Siddhartha bid his sleeping wife and son a silent farewell and departed. After crossing the border of his father's kingdom and instructing his faithful retainer to return to the palace with the horses, Siddhartha replaced his rich robes with the rough dress of a pilgrim and set out alone in pursuit of liberation.

For the next six years, Siddhartha threw himself into the search for truth. However, none of the elaborate systems he encountered—materialism, nihilism, eternalism, dualism—was convincing. Nor did the quietism of the higher states of meditation or the austerities of yoga resolve his doubts. Near death from his dreadful ascetic practices, skeleton-thin and with a complexion the color of cremation ashes, Siddhartha collapsed next to a river outside the village of Gaya. After dragging himself into the water and washing away the years of grime, Siddhartha broke his fast by accepting a nutritious gruel of milk-rice from a village girl. His health restored, Siddhartha sat resolutely beneath a large tree, vowing to be enlightened or die. That night, the forces of darkness—fear, doubt, lust—mounted an all-out assault, but the determined Siddhartha held firm. Upon seeing the morning star, Siddhartha attained supreme and perfect enlightenment; he was totally awakened, a being full of wisdom and free of illusion: a Buddha.

During the following forty-nine days, Buddha abided in the bliss of nirvana. The supreme gods Brahma and Indra sensed his great enlightenment and urged him to reveal his all-embracing knowledge—knowledge that was hidden even from them—to the world. Buddha was hesitant. How could he explain such a profound realization? Would anyone understand it? Furthermore, as he knew from his own quest, wisdom is not communicable. One can be a guide, perhaps, but awakening only comes from within, never from without. The two gods pleaded with Buddha, arguing that even if many are mired in the mud, blinded by ignorance and greed, some are like budding lotus flowers ready to receive the rays of the sun, and his teaching would therefore not be in vain. Finally, Buddha acceded.

Thus Buddha began his proclamation of the Dharma, or Law, for the sake of all sentient beings, ever mindful of the paradox of teaching what cannot be taught, expressing what cannot be expressed. Throughout his fifty years of preaching, every talk Buddha gave was tailored to the mental capacity and present circumstance of his audience, differing each time in content as well as import. At the request of some followers, he instituted an order of monks and, later, nuns to provide them with a structured framework in which to practice, but he warned them that it was merely a raft to be abandoned when no longer needed. Although Buddha had no doctrine, he presented certain basic teachings in order to facilitate the practice of the Way.

The Four Noble Truths were formulated to show that (1) ordinary life is inadequate, incomplete, and unsatisfactory, with physical and mental anguish the common lot of every being; (2) such ill is caused by craving—craving not only for food, sex, wealth, and domination but also for ideas, set theories, and hard-and-fast beliefs; (3) craving can be eliminated by casting off attachments, casting off limiting thoughts and opinions, and casting off all notions of self; (4) the best way to eradicate suffering and craving is the Eightfold Path: proper understanding, proper thought, proper speech, proper action, proper livelihood, proper effort, proper mindfulness, and proper meditation.

All conditioned things share Three Marks: impermanence, imperfection, and non-substantiality. Everything flows in an endless stream. Everywhere there is pain, turmoil, confusion, and unrest. No place is there an enduring self. If all decays, why chase after material things? If life is suffering, why not seek true bliss? If there is no abiding personality, why cling to ego?

The Wheel of Life describes the ceaseless whirl of existence: ignorance of reality leads to willful acts; willful acts lead to conscious discrimination; conscious discrimination leads to name and form; name and form lead to sense perception; sense perception leads to contact; contact leads to desire; desire leads to clinging;

clinging leads to becoming; becoming leads to birth; birth leads to old age and death. As long as there is ignorance, the cycle of birth and death revolves. Root out ignorance through practice, and the Wheel of Life will cease to spin.

Buddha instructed his followers to tread the Middle Way by avoiding any type of physical, psychological, or philosophical extreme. The Middle Way is more than simple moderation; it signifies the flexibility, openness, and freedom that is found when one is centered between all poles of opposition.

Due to the tremendous depth and breadth of Buddha's teaching, his disciples, during his life and afterwards, tended to focus on one particular aspect. Those who thought the precepts most important codified and carefully observed the monastic regulations; those who thought his Dharma talks essential memorized, collected, and studied his words; those who considered him a master of logical analysis organized complex systems of rational idealism; those who perceived his meditation as the key passed their days sitting quietly in remote areas; those who felt his compassion to be the heart of the teaching worked in the world serving all sentient beings; those who heard him say, "What I have taught is like the few leaves in my hand; what I know but have not told you is like the leaves in this great forest," sought out the mysteries hinted at and discovered countless esoteric teachings; and finally, there were those who did not see him as a human being at all, but as an embodiment of transcendental wisdom worthy of the grandest philosophical speculation.

There were plenty of others who reacted less admirably to the presence of a fully enlightened one in their midst. Monks were constantly misbehaving, necessitating the promulgation of countless petty rules; schisms were created by a few demanding that everyone else use the same language or eat the same food; endless debates ensued over who possessed the "true" transmission; a jealous relative tried to assassinate Buddha and take over the order; in short, the number of charlatans, hypocrites, and scoundrels always equaled, if not surpassed, the number of enlightened saints and sages.

Buddha passed away at eighty surrounded by his disciples (among whom was his son). His last injunctions were: "Everything decays, train with diligence" and "Rely on yourselves, no one else!"

Linear-minded historians contend that Buddhism gradually developed—or degenerated, depending on the view—into countless forms as it spread throughout Asia. But actually, all of the main elements, positive and negative, that constitute the phenomenon known as Buddhism were present right from the beginning, continually expressed in new ways and borrowed forms, it is true, but always essentially the same, not bound to any one place or era. The message is as clear as ever, and the challenges and rewards of Buddhist practice remain undiminished.

POINTS TO WATCH IN BUDDHIST TRAINING   In the Buddhist scheme of things, there are no random events; every meeting is significant whether one realizes it at the time or not, the product of *innen,* the infinitely complex web of karmic relationships. The full dimensions of innen are not readily comprehensible (only a Buddha, it is said, can fathom it in its entirety) but its presence cannot be denied. Is there anyone whose life has not been altered by some seemingly chance encounter? Regardless of the motivation, the act of picking up this book and reading this sentence is innen. Who knows where it will lead?

The desire to learn about Buddhism, known as *hosshin* in Japanese, originates in *in,* the inner cause. The direction of one's study and practice follows *en,* the outer factors—the special bonds formed among one's teachers, fellow practitioners, and acquaintances. Since those bonds differ for each and every person, no one teaching, no single way, is right for everyone. Inner cause provides the impetus, outer factors the framework. Taken together, they form innen, the cosmic links of Buddhist practice.

Everyone possesses the seed of awakening, but it will not bear fruit if it is not cultivated. Any act, deed, or exercise that enables one to uncover his or her innate Buddha nature is a *gyō*, a spiritual practice. Gyō is not to be thought of as asceticism or self-torture. It is a forging of the body and mind, a wearing away of the rough edges. *Shugyō,* extended periods of "hard training," is necessary to bring the inner realities into focus. The purpose of shugyō is to foster mindfulness, total attention to the matter at hand.

The two types of training session most frequently offered to the public are *zazenkai,* which may last several hours, and *sesshin,* intense periods of Zen training that may last up to one week. Initially, hard training in either short or longer doses involves a large measure of physical and mental pain. It takes time to grind away impurities accumulated over the years. With perseverance, the discomfort eventually disappears, but one must not lapse into a self-satisfied trance. Hard training is of no value if not accompanied by a deepening of one's insight and an expanding of one's compassion.

At the outset of your training, be a seeker: practice at many different places, meet a variety of teachers, do not be afraid to challenge yourself. Eventually, however, it is necessary to settle on the practice that seems right for you; it does not truly matter which path you ultimately select, but it cannot be a forced or unnatural choice. If you are uncomfortable with a particular method after making a serious attempt to appreciate it, or have outgrown certain forms, give them up without regret. There must be no strain, no pushing at the higher levels of practice. When the daily acts of life and enlightened practice are one, that is Buddhism.

Buddhist practice must be approached with an open and flexible mind; anyone with romantic fantasies or neat academic theories will either be sorely disappointed or rudely shocked once he or she faces the realities of practice. Background reading is important, but it must be realized that all presentations of Buddhism, even in the sutras, are inadequate attempts to fix in words what cannot be fixed. Try to refrain from cataloging people, places, events, and your own reactions. Be receptive, expand your horizons, but never suspend your critical faculties. As Buddha told his followers, "Believe nothing just because you have been told it, or because it is commonly held, or because it is a tradition, or because you thought it up yourself. Do not believe what your teacher tells you merely out of respect for the teacher. After thorough examination and analysis, whatever you find to be conducive to the good, the benefit, and the welfare of all beings—that you should believe and take as your guide." In short, do not believe anything you hear or read—including anything in this book—until you go see for yourself.

Whenever you join others in training, you become a member of the sangha, the community of Buddhist practitioners. (One of the advantages of practicing in Japan is that, in most cases, conversion to the religion or even acceptance of Buddhist tenets is not a prerequisite, nor are you under the threat of eternal damnation if you leave.) The community of practitioners is never a community of saints; in a religious sense, everyone there is "ill," afflicted with one spiritual malady or another, and some can be quite seriously disturbed. Practitioners are taking the cure of concentrated introspection in a well-ordered environment. While the leader of the group will generally be wise and venerable, his disciples can be crude, ignorant, and petty.

The quality of enlightened guidance varies. Outright charlatans are fairly rare, but even the best teachers have trouble distinguishing between essential Buddhism and the customs of Japanese Buddhism. Tradition weighs heavily on most, and many things are done simply because "they have always been done like that." Many masters have weaknesses for costly robes and fancy titles; some are heavy smokers and drinkers; a few espouse the most extreme right-wing politics; and the majority have high estimations of their own worth: "I am the only one who understands Buddhism" is sure to be heard more than once.

Whatever the shortcomings or limitations of your teachers, if they inspire and bring out the best in you, they are good masters. When dealing with any master or teacher apply the Middle Way: respect, not worship, impartial evaluation, not judgment by impossible standards.

The sangha and its leaders never form a utopian society of awakened ones; Buddhist practice never occurs outside the realities of life, realities that are the same inside and outside the temple walls. Yet is it not true that the roughest stone, rubbed continually against other equally rough stones, gradually becomes a smooth, lustrous gem?

PRACTICAL MATTERS   This book is geared to those who want to learn by doing. While the individual listings provide essential information, details must be obtained first-hand. If you lack formal experience of Buddhist meditation or are new to Japan or otherwise unsure about your direction, start with those places that provide specifically for beginners and newcomers. Become thoroughly accustomed to basic procedures before moving farther afield or undertaking advanced studies. Some general comments follow.

There can be a language barrier. Japanese is a difficult tongue to master, and the written language, one of the world's most challenging, can keep all but the keenest students illiterate. Fortunately, instruction in English is now widely available so the problem is not insurmountable. To avoid unnecessary misunderstandings and complications, do not attempt to study at a Japanese-only center until you have a solid command of the language, or unless you are accompanied by a bilingual friend. Once you can handle Japanese well you can train almost anywhere.

There are a number of Japanese language schools in Tokyo and Kyoto but they are rather expensive. There is no substitute for hard, independent study in learning a foreign language.

Most temples and other places have a standard fee for overnight training sessions. At present, such fees generally range from ¥2,000 to ¥3,000 a day, including meals. For those places with no set schedule of fees, a similar amount should be offered as a donation. When making such a donation be sure to put the money in an envelope first.

The listings give a general idea of current fees for most of the places, but be sure to check for the latest rates before attending any session. If accepted as a trainee, it is possible to live at a full-time temple very cheaply. The amount depends on the circumstances, however, and is negotiated prior to assuming residency.

In most places, any kind of modest, loose-fitting, comfortable clothing of subdued color is acceptable. Serious practitioners generally prefer to wear a kimono or martial art uniform with a *hakama* skirt to meditation sessions. The set can be had for from ¥15,000 to ¥20,000. Jewelery or perfume in the meditation hall is inappropriate. It is a good idea to bring along a pair of sandals. *Zōri,* Japanese-style sandals (with white, not black, bands), are best. In addition to removing your shoes prior to entering a temple or meditation hall, remove your socks.

Not surprisingly, the food in temples and shukubo is Japanese: miso soup, pickles, buckwheat noodles, and, generally, white rice, although a few places serve brown rice (*gemmai*). You are unable to state your preference, of course. Following the example of Buddha, everything put into one's bowl must be gratefully received and consumed. While the food prepared during training sessions is nearly always free of meat or fish, aside from formal occasions anything can be, and is, eaten. This, too, is in accordance with Buddha's precedent. He ate everything and refused to make vegetarianism compulsory.

Sakè, known as *hannya tō* ("hot water of transcendental wisdom"), is the favorite drink of practitioners of all schools, frequently savored as "the best of all medicines." Foreign trainees are often dismayed to discover that few Buddhists here are vegetarian teetotalers. Regarding food and drink, gratitude, rather than abstinence, is emphasized in Japanese Buddhism—anything received with heartfelt thanks and sincere intent becomes a pure and wholesome food.

Anyone may attend weekly meetings and overnight training sessions open to the public. If you speak Japanese well or are accompanied by a Japanese friend, it is quite all right to simply show up for regular weekly meetings. For overnight training sessions, it will be necessary to apply beforehand, usually by phone or postcard. For longer training periods be sure to bring along comfortable work clothes, fresh underwear, and toiletries (including towels and shampoo). At a training session, you are likely to share a Japanese-style room with several other participants and sleep on *futon* mattresses.

If you plan to visit a temple for a specific reason (for example, to consult with a priest, request permission to study full time, or stay overnight at times other than public sessions) make contact by letter first and then confirm the appointment by phone a week or so later. You cannot be sure that an English speaker will answer the phone; if you do not speak Japanese, have a bilingual friend call for you. Remember common courtesy: if you just turn up outside of "business hours" you may be turned away, with good reason.

Outstanding elder Zen priests are referred to as *rōshi,* or "master." (We have referred to priests of other sects as "Reverend" in English.) The most common form of address for a chief priest (*jūshoku*) is "Hōjō-san," or "Mr. Abbot." This is the best and most convenient way of addressing the head of a Zen temple. (When a bunch of Hōjō-sans get together, they call each other by the names of their respective temples, for example, "Rinnōji-san.") The abbot's assistants and disciples are addressed by their priestly rather than family names: for instance, "Wakō-san" instead of "Takahashi-san."

A priest's rank can be determined by the color of his surplice: basic black for novices, solid colors such as brown, gray, and dull gold for chief priests, and bright brocade for important abbots. The full surplice (*kesa*) is for formal occasions; the apron-like *rakusu*—which is also worn by those who have taken lay vows— is for everyday use.

A note on hairstyles: trainees in monasteries shave their heads every few days; chief priests of family temples generally sport a modified crewcut; scholar-priests employed as professors often let their hair grow and wear suits.

Every training center is unique, with its own brand of Buddhist practice. Be observant, be polite, be sincere, obey directions carefully and cheerfully, use common sense, and you will be welcome anywhere.

Many observers here, including a large number of Buddhist priests, believe that real Buddhism is dying out in Japan and the future of Buddhism lies in the West. There are several big centers in the United States and Europe that rival, if not actually surpass in terms of size and quality of practice, anything in Asia, so it is no longer necessary to travel to the Orient to study Buddhism. Nonetheless, because of the difficulty of liberating oneself from ingrained habits and inhibiting social pressures, it is sometimes advisable to make a clean break. Excess material and spiritual baggage must be left behind.

Furthermore, the presence of earnest foreigners has had a beneficial effect on the Japanese; it sparks renewed interest in Buddhism and goads native practitioners not to be outshone by their blue-eyed brothers.

It is quite difficult to make proper arrangements from abroad because most places are understandably hesitant to make a long-term commitment without conducting a personal interview or subjecting an applicant to a trial period. It is preferable to have an introduction from an overseas organization with contacts in Japan. However, if you do not have such an introduction, the best method to follow is to travel to Japan on a tourist visa (Americans are issued short-term visas but many nationalities can stay for up to six months without a visa; check with the local Japanese consulate), visit the centers of your choice (after making the proper arrangements of course), and then select a suitable place to train.

If you decide to continue your practice, you will need an appropriate visa. Temple sponsorship is always on a case-by-case basis. Sponsorship will be found, however, for anyone who has demonstrated his or her sincerity. After submitting the required documents and receiving official approval for a new visa, you will have to leave Japan, either returning home or making a short trip to Korea, Hong Kong, or Bangkok to get a new visa. Bring plenty of money. As mentioned previously, charges are reasonable in the temples, but outside lodging and travel are expensive, and you will need sufficient funds to cover the trip outside Japan to acquire a new visa. Do not expect to earn money teaching English—that is not permitted on a tourist visa.

Do not come in winter. Those from warmer areas and those accustomed to central heating will freeze in the unheated temples and meditation halls—no socks or extra clothing are allowed. (The initial winter of training is an unpleasant shock, but after a few seasons of cold-weather practice one gradually learns to appreciate the cleansing, invigorating qualities of the frosty air.) Otherwise the climate is temperate, though some are made ill by the constant humidity.

SOME FRIENDLY ADVICE   Sad to say, the current state of Japanese Buddhism is not what it should be. Buddhist priests here have a well-deserved reputation for greed, and not a few are little more than confidence men, demanding outrageous fees for funerals and other dubious services. At the other extreme, there are the caretaker priests who maintain their temples as museums. Make no mistake, much of what you will encounter is sham Buddhism. However, if you exercise caution and keep searching for the real thing, sooner or later you will find it.

In some places women are treated basically the same as men, but in the older, more conservative centers women have second-class status, being made to act as seamstresses and maids. At other places they are not welcome at all. We have indicated in the listings the places that are not suitable for women practitioners.

Those who want to practice full-time at a Japanese center must adjust to the Japanese pecking order. Anyone who precedes you in a group, even by a day, is your senior (*sempai*) and you are always the junior (*kōhai*), bound to address the senior properly and meekly follow his or her every bidding. Egalitarian-minded foreigners almost never like the system, but if you argue or otherwise rebel you will get nowhere. The senior-junior system is something that must be stoically borne. It does have certain advantages; since everyone knows his place things run more smoothly, and good seniors do more than simply order juniors around—they provide moral support and careful guidance.

The worst tendency among foreigners studying in Japan is the delusion that a few months, or even a few days, of training somehow qualifies them as "experts" or "teachers." One fellow we came across, here for a brief 100-day training session, related to us how he had already selected his "Dharma-heir" from among his followers back in the U.S. Such rank beginners love to boast of the many weeks spent in some temple or the wonderful year with Master So-and-So. Because of the time and visa limitations, most places waive the customary waiting period—in the old days a minimum of three years—for foreigners, and offer them advanced instruction right away, thus creating a false impression of substantial progress.

No matter how much time you have devoted to training, there is still more to learn. It is not unusual to hear a good teacher refer to a disciple with ten years of hard training as a "new face." Always maintain a beginner's mind, and you will avoid the pitfall of being a self-designated expert.

There are several Christian Zen groups here and quite a few Christian ministers and Catholic religious—Jesuits, especially, go for Zen in a big way—who regularly participate in zazenkai and sesshin. All of this is fine as far as it goes, and anyone may use the mechanism of meditation to enhance one's spiritual life. However, we suggest that the reader accept Buddhism on its own terms and forget, at least temporarily, about combining the two approaches.

1. Calligraphy reading "All you encounter is a vehicle for training." Whatever we come into contact with, wherever we find ourselves, is a *dōjō,* a place of training and enlightenment. By Zuiun (d. 1870). Private collection.

2. Zen monks taking a meal. Eating is an extension of meditation practice and must be done "mindfully." (Shun'ei Suyama, courtesy of Soto Zen Headquarters)

3. The richly embroidered *kesa* (surplice) of this Zen *rōshi* in full regalia indicates his high rank. The staff in his right hand and the fly whisk in his left are symbols of his authority as a teacher. (Jose Caldeira)

4. These two pages from a pilgrim's *nōkyōchō,* a kind of passport, are inscribed or stamped at each temple he or she visits.

5. In a typical scene from a *zazenkai,* a Zen meditation meeting open to the public, the sitter on the left has requested the monitor to strike his shoulders with the *keisaku* stick. (Kyodo-FPC Japan)

6. *Shōjin ryōri*, "food for practice," often consists of many delicately prepared vegetarian dishes served with care and style. (Kyodo-FPC Japan).

PART ONE

MEDITATION AND STUDY

A NOTE TO THE READER   Entries are grouped by geographical area. Some temples are listed more than once, for it is possible that basic training, ordination, Buddhist vegetarian fare, and temple accommodations may all be offered at one place. For convenience, multiple appearances are cross-referenced, and an alphabetical finding list has been provided.

Tokyo Area

The nation's capital and its surrounding vicinity have never been regarded as a major center for Buddhist practice, but because of the city's size and importance it has naturally attracted many groups and institutions. The Sōtō sect of Zen is well represented here, for its administrative headquarters are located in Tokyo. In addition, Sōjiji in neighboring Yokohama is a major center of Sōtō practice and one of the two head temples of the sect.

As Japan's business and political center, Tokyo is home for many foreigners, and various people have tried to start English-language groups to offer guidance in meditation and Buddhist studies to those who do not speak Japanese. It is ironic that in this respect Tokyo can probably offer more to the beginner not fluent in Japanese than can Kyoto, the center of Japanese Buddhism.

One drawback of these English-language groups, however, is that they often revolve around the enthusiasm of a single person, and may collapse quickly when he or she returns home, moves to a remote monastery, or is otherwise no longer able to exercise leadership. The groups featured below, some of which have lasted several years, appear destined to continue. Still, be warned that they may no longer exist by the time you arrive in Japan. You may cherish the comfort that others will almost certainly have taken their place. The best source of information is the "Announcements" column of the *Japan Times,* and similar columns in Japan's three other English-language dailies: the *Mainichi Daily News,* the *Daily Yomiuri,* and the *Asahi Evening News.* These also sometimes list lectures in English on different aspects of Japanese and Asian Buddhism, sponsored by local cultural associations. The government-sponsored Tourist Information Center (TIC) also keeps a listing of temples open to foreigners. Keep in mind, too, that dozens of Zen temples in Tokyo offer regular zazenkai for local residents. These are usually at times to suit working people—early morning and in the evening—and are, of course, entirely in Japanese. There will usually be no objection to a foreigner attending, however, and in many cases you may even find yourself subject to an enthusiastic welcome. Various publications in Japanese such as *Zazen no Susume* published by the Institute for Zen Studies in Kyoto (see page 40) list many of these local zazenkai, and the Sōtō Zen headquarters will supply a directory of their sect's zazenkai upon request. For other lists, those who read Japanese may turn to books in the Buddhism section that can be found in most large book stores.

Kamakura is one of Japan's historic centers of Zen Buddhism, just an hour by train from central Tokyo. For the foreign tourist it has less to offer than Kyoto—it is not as old and its buildings are neither as grand nor as famous—yet it is well worth a visit. Unlike Kyoto, it is a compact city that has managed to resist industrialization and has retained much of its natural beauty. In addition to its religious heritage, it has been the home of many famous writers and artists through the centuries.

Kamakura is perhaps best known today for its magnificent Great Buddha. Also here are the great Rinzai temples Engakuji and Kenchōji, both founded in the thirteenth century. At their peak, they were the center of a flourishing Zen culture, but today are better known as tourist attractions than as Zen training institutions. In fact, unlike Kyoto, where many of the major temples at least offer regular zazenkai, Kamakura is surprisingly restrictive to outsiders, and it is difficult to practice there without introductions from Japanese priests. Perhaps the reason for this is the city's proximity to Tokyo and its reputation as an exotic spot for day-trippers, leading the temples to "batten down the hatches." Nevertheless, foreigners who can demonstrate sufficient sincerity, including Japanese language ability and previous Zen study, will find some doors open to them.

The Tokyo TIC is near the Tōhō Twin Tower Building, not far from Hibiya, Yūrakuchō, or Ginza stations, at 1–6–6 Yūrakuchō, Chiyoda-ku, Tokyo 100. Tel: (03) 502–1461.

ツーリスト・インフォーメィション・センター　千代田区有楽町 1–6–6

TAISŌJI　　　Taisōji offers foreigners in Tokyo the chance to practice regular zazen, with instruction in English from Ann Sargent, an American woman who came to Japan in 1978 and has since become a Sōtō Zen nun. She organizes early-morning zazen every day except Sunday, and anyone is welcome to attend. She is happy to help beginners, and this is an excellent place for those in the Tokyo area who speak little Japanese and wish to begin studying Zen.

Ann herself studied and practiced Zen in Los Angeles, under Matsunaga Rōshi, a Japanese Sōtō priest who spent twenty years in Brazil, Hawaii, and California before returning to Japan to take over administration of his family's country temple in Shizuoka Prefecture, southwest of Tokyo. Ann followed him to Japan in 1978 to resume her studies, while organizing a Zen center at her home and working part-time as a technical writer, her work for twenty years in California. In mid-1984 she moved to an apartment near Taisōji, and began to teach Zen there instead of in her home.

The time for zazen is not fixed. Ann is prepared, to some extent, to arrange it around the particular schedules of those attending, and has even organized afternoon sittings for certain groups, and is hoping to begin regular evening practice as well. She is also the organizer of a monthly zazenkai for foreigners at Taisōji. This group usually meets on the last Sunday of the month, and anyone is welcome; it is especially suitable for beginners. Each meeting usually consists of about forty-five minutes of zazen, followed by a talk in English by Matsunaga Rōshi on some aspect of Zen. Up to twenty people attend each time. Occasionally Ann or another in the group arranges for a stay at a country temple, including a weekend sesshin at Matsunaga Rōshi's temple.

This zazenkai is listed each month in the "Announcements" column of the *Japan Times* and similar columns in other English newspapers. Anyone is welcome, without prior notice, though it is advisable to phone Ann first for precise directions. First-timers should arrive a little early for instruction in the correct method of sitting and other procedures. As much as possible, the group tries to follow the procedures of Sōtō monasteries. Thus there is a set procedure for walking into the zendō, for laying one's meditation cushion (*zafu*) on the tatami, and for sitting, accompanied by several bows in various directions. It is not difficult, but it can be slightly confusing for those without experience.

Despite the formalities, the zazenkai is basically a friendly and relaxed affair, with priests and participants, the latter often in jeans and T-shirts, chatting over tea and cookies before returning home. Many are regulars who have advanced to deeper study, while others, some of them tourists attracted by the newspaper announcement, attend only once.

Ann lives at Sōmei Kōpo 104, 7-1-30 Komagome, Toshima-ku, Tokyo 170. Tel: (03) 940-0979. Taisōji is at 7-1-1 Komagome, Toshima-ku, Tokyo 170. Tel: (03) 917-4477. (The temple can be contacted in Japanese only.) Both are a ten-minute walk from Sugamo station on the Toei Mita subway and the Yamanote lines. The address of Matsunaga Rōshi's temple is Sōtokuin, Okitsuhon-chō, Shimizu-shi, Shizuoka-ken 424. Tel: (0543) 69-2244.

泰宗寺　豊島区駒込 7-1-1

松永然道　静岡県清水市興津本町　宗徳院

NISHIJIMA GROUP   Businessman-priest Gudō Wafū Nishijima has for many years taken an active interest in helping Westerners who wish to study and practice Zen in Tokyo. As well as conducting a weekly English-language zazenkai he has organized sesshin for foreigners, has taken on foreign disciples, and has made himself available for consultation in English with people who wish to discuss Zen. He says that foreigners often make better students than do Japanese because of their open minds to the subject, free of prejudices. He also finds many foreigners more sincere about their involvement in Zen. He emphasizes that a person who wants to study Zen should concentrate on two things, zazen and a study of Buddhist theory. "The essence of Zen is practicing zazen," he says. "It can be done anywhere, including in one's own home." He feels that many people who visit exotic temples to practice are really more interested in sightseeing, and states that Buddhist theory can be studied from the many books on the subject. "Buddhist theory is really a very clear and exact system of thought," he contends. "It is possible to give definite answers to all questions. I am happy to help anyone with problems."

As a young man Nishijima Rōshi studied various philosophies, but found himself attracted to the notion, inherent in Buddhism, that by action, not by thought, man can save himself. He began to read the *Shōbōgenzō* by Dōgen as well as commentaries on it, and gradually found himself starting to grasp the deeper meaning. He recalls: "After I had understood it, and by practicing zazen, I grew confident that Buddhism is the ultimate philosophy for the world, even for the Western world."

He graduated in law from Tokyo University and joined a finance company as an auditor, but continued his Buddhist training, becoming a priest, though with special dispensation from his teacher to hold a secular job. Now he has retired and is working as a consultant for a small cosmetics company, whose president is one of his disciples. Among his duties are the organization of a regular zazenkai for the staff.

In 1969 Nishijima Rōshi began conducting weekly zazenkai for the Young Men's Buddhist Association of Tokyo University, and three years later began lecturing in English. Today he holds a zazenkai for foreigners (men and women are both welcome) on the first, third, and fifth Saturdays of the month on the seventh floor of the Nihon Shimpan Building and on the fourth Saturday on the seventh floor of the Buddhist Promoting Foundation. Regular announcements telling the time and location are in the announcement columns of Tokyo's English-language papers.

He also organizes regular sesshin at a tranquil Sōtō mountain temple in Shizuoka Prefecture, southwest of Tokyo. Most of the participants are Japanese, but a few foreigners regularly join, and others are welcome, even beginners. In September 1982 he conducted a sesshin for the first time entirely in English, and repeated this a year later. He expects his yearly September sesshin in English to continue. Altogether, he organizes five annual sesshin, in May, June, August, September, and October. They each last two nights and three days, apart from the August sesshin, which is three nights and four days. Zazen is conducted four times daily at these sesshin, with new students allowed to stretch their legs occasionally, and even retire to their rooms for short spells if they find their bodies aching too much.

Nishijima Rōshi has written several introductions to Buddhist study and practice in Japanese and two in English, *How to Practice Zazen* (Bukkyōsha) and *To Meet the Real Dragon* (Wind-bell Publications).

The Nihon Shimpan Building is at 3–33–5 Hongō, Bunkyō-ku, Tokyo 113, near the Hongō Sanchōme station on the Marunouchi subway line and a ten-minute walk from Tokyo University. For the Buddhist Promoting Foundation see page 12. Nishijima Rōshi can be contacted during business hours at (03) 235–0701 or at home at (0429) 98–6092.

西嶋和夫座禅会　文京区本郷 3–33–5 日本信販ビル

BUDDHIST ENGLISH ACADEMY   The Buddhist English Academy was founded by a group of priests, students, and others who wanted to help English-speaking delegates to the twelfth General Conference of the World Fellowship of Buddhists, held in Tokyo in 1978. After the conference, the group decided to keep the Academy going, in order to promote Buddhism abroad and to assist foreigners in studying Buddhism in Japan. Today the Academy is thriving, with an office that you can contact in English and a highly diversified program. Meetings are every Friday night, from 6:30 to 8:30, at Jōenji, a Nichiren temple in the night-life district of Shinjuku. Priests and academics who comprise the Academy's board of directors take turns delivering English-language lectures. One of the regular speakers is the Rev. Masao Ichishima, leader of the Zen'yōji Seminars (p.10).

The Academy also organizes a regular speech contest as well as numerous field trips, some of which take the participants to temples and other holy places not normally open to the public. These can include several days of religious training at Enryakuji on Mt. Hiei, a tour of remote country Zen temples, and visits to temples in famous tourist resorts like Kamakura and Nikkō with lunch at a shōjin ryōri restaurant. Sometimes the Academy organizes trips in conjunction with local organizations of foreigners. Participants are usually divided equally between foreigners and Japanese. The latter include students, office workers, priests, and others. You can expect to pay a fee for all activities to cover expenses; details are always announced in advance.

The Academy is an excellent fount of information for those interested in both theoretical and practical aspects of Buddhism, at all levels. It has contacts with all the main Buddhist sects and with a wide spectrum of Buddhist organizations. It can even tailor programs to the particular interests of a group, and is a good contact point for foreigners newly arrived in Japan or for those abroad who wish to research some field of Japanese Buddhism.

The Secretary General of the Academy is the Rev. Enshin Saitō, a young Tendai priest. The office is at 802 Diamond Palace, 3–5–3 Nishi Shinjuku, Shinjuku-ku, Tokyo 160. Tel: (03) 342–6605.

仏教英語研究会　新宿区西新宿 3–5–3 ダイヤモンドパレス 802

ZEN'YŌJI SEMINARS   In 1979 the Reverend Masao Ichishima, a Tendai priest and dean of academic affairs at Tokyo's Taishō University, a Buddhist institution, was asked to give a lecture in English and conduct meditation for a group of foreigners at Zen'yōji, a Tendai temple near the university. He was very well received and subsequently found himself asked to return. The seminars have continued ever since, usually between 6:00 and 8:30 P.M. on the last Tuesday of the month. A typical seminar consists of a one-hour lecture, a thirty-minute discussion, and twenty-four minutes of meditation (twenty-four minutes being the ideal time for meditation for a beginner, according to an eighth-century Tibetan text).

Most of the lectures are on the theme of Zen or Tantric Buddhism, but other subjects may include Tibetan Buddhism, on which the Rev. Ichishima is an authority, or such subjects as Buddhist art or the eighty-eight-temple pilgrimage of Shikoku. The Rev. Ichishima has the uncommon ability to explain the most difficult Buddhist terms in easy layman's English, coupled with anecdotes, jokes, and some fascinating stories, and these seminars are highly recommended. Both Japanese and foreigners attend regularly, with some thirty-five foreigners turning up for one seminar on moonlight meditation. There is no charge.

The Rev. Ichishima spent three years in Hawaii as assistant bishop to the Tendai mission to the islands. While there he organized a Buddhist English translation society under the auspices of the University of Hawaii. He also launched a course at the university in Tibetan Buddhism. He next spent two years at the University of California in Berkeley doing research in Oriental languages, and also taught at the university's Institute of Buddhist Studies.

During this time he helped Californian Buddhists inaugurate a mountain pilgrimage on Mount Tamalpais near San Francisco, based on pilgrimages on Japan's Mount Hiei. "I told them which places on the route to use for worship," he recalls. "For instance, if I found a very auspicious rock I would say they should stop there to pray and chant some mantras." (The Rev. Ichishima also claims to have devised for his own purposes what he calls "commuting Zen," to cope with the 1½-hour train journey between his home and work, most of it spent strap-hanging. He states: "I worked out the best posture—a straight back and square but relaxed shoulders—and now I take some deep breaths and start meditating when the train sets off. The next thing I know, I have arrived at my destination, fresh and relaxed.")

Concerning his seminars, he says he wants to help everyone from abroad learn about real Buddhism and Oriental culture. He will do this on a non-sectarian basis. He notes that the big problem for most foreigners is that they don't speak Japanese, and he feels that he is in a position to help them overcome this difficulty. He has arranged introductions with English-speaking priests for visiting academics and others, has invited to his own country temple in Chiba Prefecture, east of Tokyo, a group of foreigners for a three-day session in moonlight meditation, and has translated into English various important Buddhist tracts and liturgies. He has done much of this in connection with the Buddhist English Academy (p. 9) with which he is closely involved.

He has also taken as disciples some foreigners who wished to become Tendai priests, has taught them at Taishō University and at his own temple, and has introduced them to training at Enryaku-ji on Mount Hiei. He says there are no particular qualifications for a person who wishes to start training to be a Tendai priest. But he stresses that the person must be sincere. "The people who became my disciples have all really wanted to be priests, so I gave them the opportunity," he states.

Zen'yōji is a small but surprisingly peaceful temple in a heavily built-up suburb of Tokyo. The address is 4–8–25 Nishi Sugamo, Toshima-ku, Tokyo 170. Tel: (03) 915–0015 (phone in Japanese only). It is a five-minute walk from Nishi Sugamo station on the Toei Mita subway line. The Rev. Masao Ichishima can be contacted at Taishō University, 3–20–1 Nishi Sugamo, Toshima-ku, Tokyo 170. Tel: (03) 918–7311.

善養寺　豊島区西巣鴨 4–8–25

大正大学　豊島区西巣鴨 3–20–1

SŌTŌ ZEN HEADQUARTERS　　The Sōtō branch of Zen has its administrative headquarters in a large, modern building near central Tokyo. From the outside, and indeed from the inside as well, there is little to indicate that this is a religious institution; it could just as easily be the head office of one of Japan's famous trading companies. Nevertheless, this is a useful source of information for those living in Tokyo. The headquarters produces a number of publications, including a few in English, such as short introductions to Zen and translations of important sutras. (These are on display at the reception desk in the lobby.) Lists of all the Sōtō temples in Japan are also available, including those with zazenkai. Many young priests work on temporary assignment in the headquarters building, and it is sometimes possible to find someone who speaks English. In the same building is the Tokyo Grand Hotel, owned by the Sōtō organization.

2–5–2 Shiba, Minato-ku, Tokyo 105. Tel: (03) 454–5411. A short walk from Shiba Kōen station on the Toei Mita subway line.

曹洞宗宗務庁　港区芝 2–5–2

BUDDHIST PROMOTING FOUNDATION　　This nondenominational organization, responsible for distributing worldwide some one million foreign-language copies of the book *The Teaching of Buddha* to date, is the child of one of Japan's most amazing entrepreneurs, eighty-six-year-old Yehan Numata, chairman of Mitsutoyo Manufacturing Company. You can learn about his life by reading *My Path,* one of the many other publications of the foundation. It is a fascinating story.

The third son of a poor family who could not afford to send him to high school, he received the chance to pursue his education in America, thanks to the support of the Jōdo Shinshū sect. After working in Hollywood for two years as a houseboy to cover his expenses, he contracted tuberculosis, a disease then considered fatal. He turned to Saint Shinran, the founder of Jōdo Shinshū, and began to recite the prayers and sutras he had learned as a child. His health recovered. Later he graduated in mathematics from the University of California in Berkeley, but decided to work for the propagation of Buddhism. For some years he helped publish literature in English for distribution in America, but was continually thwarted by lack of funds, which led him to the conclusion that he should start his own firm to ensure a regular income. In 1934 Mitsutoyo was born.

Today the company is one of the world's leading makers of precision instruments. It operates manufacturing subsidiaries in Brazil and the U.S. and has offices in many other countries, which double as branches of the Buddhist Promoting Foundation. Mr. Numata's own income, from company dividends and from royalties on the more than twenty patents he holds, comes to some $1.7 million per year, which he gives to the foundation for its activities.

The foundation publishes *The Teaching of Buddha* in Japanese, English, and numerous other languages, and distributes it free to hotels around the world. Any hotel wishing copies will freely receive one for each room, with replacements sent every three months. A pamphlet from the foundation reproduces grateful acknowledgments from guests and hotel managers at such institutions as the Hotel Westminster in Nice, France, the Sao Paulo Hilton in Brazil, and the Gala Hotel in Taipei, Taiwan. The Foundation also distributes a variety of other Buddhist literature in

English, cassette tapes, and some art works. Recently Mr. Numata also inaugurated in the foundation's building a restaurant serving Chinese-style Buddhist vegetarian dishes with the aim of promoting vegetarianism. For further information see Bodaiju (p. 97).

4–3–14 Shiba, Minato-ku, Tokyo 108. Tel: (03) 455–5851. A few people there speak English. It is near Mita station on the Toei Mita subway line and Tamachi station on the Yamanote line.

仏教伝道協会　港区芝 4–3–14

TŌSHŌJI   Like many Zen temples, Tōshōji offers regular early-morning zazen. But it is probably unique in Tokyo in that for many years it has also offered rooms for people who wish to experience life in a Zen temple without pursuing full-time Zen studies. Consequently, many foreigners have stayed here. Some are tourists, while others are working or studying in the capital, and live there for up to two or three years. It must be stressed, though, that Tōshōji is not a hostel or some kind of crash pad. It is a Sōtō Zen temple, and your primary purpose for seeking to stay there must be to practice zazen. All residents must get up by 5:00 each morning for exercises and zazen. This is followed at 5:30 by half an hour of sutra chanting (with Roman-letter sutra sheets available) and one hour devoted to cleaning the premises. Breakfast is at 7:00, and afterwards guests are free to follow their own pursuits. Rates are extremely reasonable. People who stay more than a month will find it cheaper than a youth hostel.

"We decided to accept boarders in order to encourage people to practice Zen," says a priest at the temple. "We have had people from many countries. We welcome them all." The temple's ten small guest rooms are quite bare, and in general you are expected to supply your own bedding. Exceptions might be possible for those staying only a short time. There are few rules. For instance, alcohol is not forbidden and there is no night curfew. But because of the temple's strict insistence on regular attendance at zazen it is necessary to follow a relatively sober way of life. Friends are not permitted to stay overnight in your room. Empty rooms are generally available but if all rooms are occupied you may find yourself forced to share with someone.

Tōshōji is a new temple, built after the war, and largely resembles the houses, shops, and offices between which it finds itself squeezed. Do not expect a quaint old wooden building; from the outside it shows none of the charm of older, country temples. Several young priests are usually living there, and if you are lucky one or more will speak some English. If not, and you do not know Japanese, you will have to do the best you can with smiles and sign language. You should telephone first to arrange your stay there.

4–5–18 Yutakachō, Shinagawa-ku, Tokyo 142. Tel: (03) 781–4235. A five-minute walk from Togoshi Kōen station on the Ōimachi line.

東照寺　品川区豊町 4–5–18

EIHEIJI TOKYO BETSUIN　　Although a training temple for Sōtō Zen monks, the Tokyo branch of Eiheiji has a weekly zazenkai open to all, every Monday from 7:00 to 9:00 P.M. It is very well known among Tokyo residents, and attracts a large attendance, usually including some foreigners. Everything is in Japanese, but easily followed instruction in how to sit will be given to beginners who phone in advance to announce their intention of attending.

Permission to attend the early morning sittings (5:00–6:00 A.M.) may be obtained, and lay people attend the two annual sesshin from February 1 to 7 and December 1 to 8. Allowances are made for working people, and it is possible to attend only part of a sesshin. The lay participants (up to twenty) sleep together in two large rooms and sit with the monks from 5:00 A.M. to 9:00 P.M.

This temple offers a good balance of friendliness with traditional formality—kind help, but no nonsense in the meditation hall—and is recommended for people at all levels.

2–21–14 Nishi Azabu, Minato-ku, Tokyo 106. Tel: (03) 400–

5232. A ten-minute walk from Roppongi station on the Hibiya subway line.

永平寺東京別院　港区西麻布 2–21–14

TESSHŪKAI　　Headed by Sōgen Ōmori, perhaps Japan's foremost Rinzai Zen master, the Tesshūkai (Tesshū Society) is one of the more dynamic places at which to practice in Tokyo. In addition to Rinzai-style zazen, punctuated with spirited shouts and vigorous application of the *keisaku* stick (on the younger trainees), there is instruction in the classical Jūbokudō school of calligraphy and Jikishin-kage Ryū swordsmanship.

Originally trained as a swordsman and calligrapher prior to his ordination as a priest in his forties, Ōmori Rōshi follows the tradition of the great nineteenth-century Zen master Tesshū Yamaoka. Due to old age and ill health he is not taking on any new students, but he still leads the training sessions on the second and fourth Sunday of each month. After a period of zazen from 10:00 to 11:00 A.M. he lectures on a Zen text. Then there is calligraphy and swordsmanship for those who wish to participate. Only Japanese is spoken but usually one or two foreign trainees and several English-speaking Japanese are on hand.

These meetings are open to everyone, and there is a nice mixture of swordsmen, young Zen monks, college students, housewives, Catholic priests, calligraphers, and foreigners. There is daily zazen (except Sunday) from 6:00 to 8:00 A.M. and 6:00 to 8:00 P.M. in the small building that serves as the combination zendō, martial arts hall, and calligraphy studio.

1–17–3 Chūō, Nakano-ku, Tokyo 164. Tel: (03) 368–0532. A ten-minute walk from Higashi Nakano station on the Chūō line.

鉄舟会　中野区中央 1–17–3

HITSUZENKAI　　Closely related to the Tesshūkai is the Hitsuzenkai, the "Society of the Way of the Zen Brush," led by Katsujō Terayama, Ōmori Rōshi's top disciple and one of his Dharma heirs. Terayama, a layman, holds classes at various places in Tokyo, including a special session at his home on the first Saturday of each month. After thirty minutes of zazen and a short lecture, there is group evaluation of famous pieces of calligraphy and calligraphy practice. Although the formal session concludes with a simple tea ceremony, there usually is a period of free discussion afterward. Everything is in Japanese, but Takeko, his wife, speaks English, and foreigners are always welcome. It is not necessary to know how to write Chinese characters to participate. Terayama Sensei has spent a lifetime studying the unique qualities of Oriental brushwork and anyone with an interest in Far Eastern art should attend one of these Saturday study sessions.

Hitsuzenkai Hombu Dōjō, 2–23–1 Ōi, Shinagawa-ku, Tokyo 140. Tel: (03) 775–6634. A ten-minute walk from Ōi station on the Keihin Tōhoku line. Coauthor John Stevens is associated with both the Tesshūkai and Hitsuzenkai.

筆禅会本部道場　品川区大井 2–23–1

INTERNATIONAL INSTITUTE FOR BUDDHIST STUDIES
This research institute houses an impressive collection of rare Buddhist texts and issues a variety of scholarly tracts in both English and Japanese. Since it is not open to the public, appointments to consult the collection are necessary.

Dr. Akira Yuyama, Secretary, 5–3–23 Toranomon, Minato-ku, Tokyo 105. Tel: (03) 434–6953. Dr. Yuyama speaks English.

国際仏教学研究所　港区虎の門 5–3–23

TIBET CULTURE CENTER　This active center, sponsored by the Dalai Lama's office in Dharmsala, India, offers a wide range of regularly scheduled programs on Tibetan language and culture, everything from cooking classes to seminars on Tantric Buddhism. The programs are generally conducted in Japanese, but the director, Pema Gyalpo, and the members of the staff speak English. They can direct you to the Tibetan lamas teaching in Japan. There is a nominal charge for programs. Membership is offered for three thousand yen a year.

Their office is at Room 1106 Gotanda Royal Heights, 14–7–5 Ōsaki, Shinagawa-ku, Tokyo 141. Tel: (03) 490–7868. Call for directions.

チベット文化研究所　品川区大崎 14–7–5 五反田ローヤル・ハイツ 1106

JŌKŪIN　Jōkūin is a small, rustic Sōtō temple in Saitama Prefecture, near Tokyo. With a thatched roof, high ceilings, and wooden beams it looks more like a farmhouse than a temple. It is set among trees and farmlands, far from the nearest roads, and is said to have been founded a thousand years ago.

The priest Daisen Asada lives there alone with his wife, but they conduct regular Zen training sessions for lay people. An American trainee priest was associated with them for some years and he began a program of inviting groups of foreigners for weekends of Zen instruction in English. When he left in 1975 these sessions continued, with Gaynor Sekimori, an Australian, often translating for the priest. They are now held about once a month, with advance notices appearing in Tokyo's English-language papers. Bookings by phone are necessary. Many of the people who attend the monthly meetings at Taisōji (p.5) also participate in the Jōkūin weekends. The fee is reasonable, and includes two delicious Buddhist vegetarian meals. Foreigners who speak Japanese can contact the priest directly and arrange to stay at other times for more intensive instruction.

A typical weekend session begins on Saturday afternoon with instruction in the correct method for zazen and also in the detailed manner of eating meals. The latter is not easy, as the temple follows a carefully prescribed routine, based on the traditional system at Eiheiji, for laying one's bowls on the table, receiving food, eating it, then stacking and wrapping the bowls. Zazen is conducted several times on Saturday and Sunday, and there is a morning service on Sunday, with a chanting of the *Heart Sutra.* Sutra sheets with the Japanese text printed in Roman letters, prepared by the Sōtō-sect headquarters, are available. An introductory talk on Zen by the priest is translated into English. Participants are also expected to do several hours of work around the temple grounds. Jōkūin is one of the only Japanese temples offering foreigners this chance to experience Zen temple life first-hand with instruction in English. It has been featured in magazine articles and television programs in Japan and abroad.

Although little more than twenty-four hours are spent there during the weekend sessions it is an excellent introduction to Zen and to temple life and discipline. A newcomer to Zen who attends will likely meet "older hands" who can recommend other temples worth a visit. Most participants leave grateful for the experience, and many who have had their first taste of Zen here have gone on to further and deeper practice elsewhere.

The temple can be contacted (in Japanese only) at 679 Kamigarako, Higashi Matsuyama-shi, Saitama-ken 355. Tel: (0493) 23–9815. To get there, take the Tōbu Tōjō train line to Higashi Matsuyama, and from there a bus heading for Kokusai Fujin Kaikan. Get off at Maruki Bijutsukan-mae.

The organizer of the weekends is Gaynor Sekimori, 1–2–11 Nishi Nippori, Arakawa-ku, Tokyo 116. Tel: (03) 891–8469.

浄空院　埼玉県東松山市上唐子 679

ゲィノー・セキモリ　荒川区西日暮里 1–2–11

SŌJIJI　In the 1960s Yokohama's Sōjiji, one of the Sōtō sect's two head monasteries, was very receptive to foreign visitors. Many Westerners lived there for varying periods, some for several years. The temple administration included a thriving Foreign Guest Department and published books in English explaining Zen doctrines and practice.

Times change. Today Sōjiji makes no special efforts to attract foreigners, and few go there to train. Men wishing to study at Sōjiji must now be ordained priests and must be prepared to stay a minimum of one year. Women are no longer admitted. New trainees can enter in March or September, though applications should be made well in advance through your teacher or temple. You cannot apply directly. A Sōjiji administrator noted that most of the foreigners who used to train there now prefer places like Hosshinji, described in the "Other Areas" section.

The Japanese university year ends in February, so each March up to ninety young graduates enter Sōjiji. About three-quarters are from Komazawa University, a Sōtō Zen institution in Tokyo, and most are the sons of priests. Those arriving in September are quite different. Seldom more than a dozen in number, they are usually older than those entering in March, and are often men who have thrown in careers as businessmen or school teachers to enter the priesthood.

Training is hard, with foreigners given no special treatment. For instance, the first week is spent doing virtually nothing but zazen, and for the first one hundred days there is absolutely no contact with the outside world, including no telephone calls, no letters, and no newspapers.

There are two sesshin each year, June 11–15 and December 1–8, and outsiders are welcome to join these. In addition, there is a special visitors' program under which anyone, male or female, can stay a maximum of two nights in a guests' wing. (A woman must arrive with at least one other person, male or female. A woman by herself will not be accepted.) Many foreigners take advantage of this, and the program is recommended for anyone who wishes to get a taste of life in a Zen monastery.

Do not expect to experience monastery life to the full if you stay only twenty-four hours, though if it is your first time to do zazen even that short period will have its effect on both your legs and your back. You will be asked to report to the temple office after lunch, and will then be taken to the visitors' zendō for some basic instruction in how to sit correctly, as well as how to conduct yourself around the temple, and then the first of many zazen sessions will begin.

Dinner is a meager ration of vegetables, rice gruel, soup, and pickles, taken in the visitors' quarters together with several priests assigned to look after guests. Sometimes these people are given this assignment on the basis of their ability to speak English, though you can by no means count on this.

You will have only a little time to yourself, and if you explore the temple you will find it a vast place, with a dozen large buildings connected to each other by long wooden passageways, some of them tunneling underground. A keep-left policy is enforced in these corridors for practical reasons—many of the up to 250 priests seem to fly about their tasks like whirling dervishes.

Visitors spend the evening sleeping in groups in rooms in the guest quarters, which are decorated with *sumi-e* ink pictures and landscape paintings. If there are enough people it may become a little cramped, but it will certainly be more comfortable than the *sōdō,* or "monks' hall," where each trainee priest has just one tatami mat to himself for sleeping, eating, and doing zazen.

Breakfast is even more frugal than dinner, and your morning will include cleaning or gardening as well as more zazen and a colorful morning service in the Buddha Hall, complete with the senior priests in their bright costumes, the sounds of sutra chanting, gongs, and bells, and the powerful smell of incense.

In the weekends many groups from companies visit the temple, and you are advised to come during the week, when there are usually fewer guests. If there are only a few of you, you may have the chance to join the priests outside the monks' hall for early-morning zazen, and you will also have more opportunities to talk with the priests assigned to look after you.

Applications to stay at Sōjiji should be made at least one week in advance, by telephone or in writing (in Japanese, in either case). For those unwilling to try even twenty-four hours there is a regular zazenkai at the temple, every Sunday, from 12:30 to 4:30 P.M.

2–1–1 Tsurumi, Tsurumi-ku, Yokohama-shi, Kanagawa-ken 230. Tel: (045) 581–6021. A five-minute walk from Tsurumi station on the Keihin Tōhoku line.

総持寺　神奈川県横浜市鶴見区鶴見 2–1–1

SAN'UN ZENDŌ　San'un Zendō is not a temple but a zendō, under the direction of Kōun Yamada Rōshi, who has many foreign disciples and who sometimes lectures overseas. He is a layman, as are most of his students, though a few are Buddhist priests and some are Catholic nuns or priests. A number of the leading members of the group are older people with a background in the Japanese naval forces or in leading positions in business. Some, including Yamada Rōshi and his assistant, Miyazaki Rōshi, speak English, which has encouraged many foreigners to do regular zazen there.

Training is strict, with regular attendance expected. As a general rule, newcomers are expected to arrive through the introduction of an established member. Practice is a mixture of Rinzai and Sōtō methods, with zazen done facing the wall, as in Sōtō, but with *kōan,* or Zen riddles, employed and a certain emphasis on satori, as in Rinzai. Nightly zazen is organized, with up to a dozen foreigners normally attending, and zazenkai are held on the second and fourth weekends of the month. At these weekend meetings Yamada Rōshi gives Zen instruction in English. New members are expected to attend a series of six introductory lectures. For foreigners these have been taped in English.

The San'un Zendō is for the serious student of Zen only, not for those who just want a taste. Being a beginner is not necessarily a disadvantage, just as you will not always find it advantageous to have had some Zen experience. It is vital that you demonstrate your sincerity and a commitment toward Zen practice. As mentioned, you should preferably arrive through the introduction of a regular member, and even then you may find it difficult to gain acceptance.

The San'un Zendō is closely associated with the Diamond Sangha in Hawaii, which is headed by Robert Aitken Rōshi.

For further information, including directions, contact Yamada Rōshi's assistant, Kan'un Miyazaki Rōshi, at 2–16–5 Komachi, Kamakura-shi, Kanagawa-ken 248. Tel: (0467) 23–2010.

三雲禅堂　神奈川県鎌倉市小町 2–16–5

ENGAKUJI　Founded in 1282, Engakuji is one of the most magnificent temples in Kamakura, and one of the leading attractions for tourists visiting the area. The huge bell was cast in 1301 (today it is designated a national treasure). The main gate was reconstructed in 1780 and houses some magnificent statues. There are numerous other buildings, though some are off-limits to the tourist, as are many of the art treasures.

The grounds of this Rinzai temple combine Kamakura's natural beauty with the graceful taste of Zen art, and have attracted many distinguished visitors. The great Zen master Daisetz Suzuki, whose writings were largely instrumental in introducing Zen to the West, spent his final years there until his death in 1966 at the age of ninety-six. The historian Sir George Sansom and the novelist Sōseki Natsume also chose to live in the temple grounds for a while.

A zazenkai is held every morning from 5:30 to 6:30, and on the second and fourth Sunday of each month, from 9:00 to 11:00 A.M. But the temple makes it difficult for you to attend, perhaps following the tradition of Zen institutions, which have often forced potential novitiates to spend days waiting in supplication at the temple gates before being accepted for training. "We have had foreigners come to our zazenkai," comments a priest. "They come and then they quickly go. Now we insist that everyone who joins should understand Japanese. They should also have a good knowledge of Zen, and be very serious about their studies." Even this is not enough. After making a formal application and attending a few trial sessions you may be rejected without explanation, despite your attempts to demonstrate your sincerity and seriousness. It seems likely that without contacts to help you it will be difficult to join. Do not expect any allowances for beginners.

Engakuji also accepts people for full-time training as priests. But first you will need to have spent some time in training, and then your teacher will have to make all the necessary arrangements.

409 Yamanouchi, Kamakura-shi, Kanagawa-ken 247. Tel: (0467) 22–0478. Next to Kita Kamakura station.

円覚寺　神奈川県鎌倉市山ノ内 409

HŌKOKUJI   This Rinzai temple is popular on the Kamakura tourist circuit for its pretty stone garden and bamboo grove, where visitors can relax and sip green tea. It is usually referred to as the Bamboo Temple. It is said to have been founded 650 years ago, and many famous artists and writers have lived in the temple compound, including the Nobel prize-winning author Yasunari Kawabata. He is said to have praised the incredible beauty and tranquility of the compound, which he compared to a remote mountain.

Today, with the boom in domestic tourism, Hōkokuji is no longer tranquil. A small shop hawks books and cassettes containing the head priest's teachings on Buddhism, and photographs around the temple show the visits of various celebrities. Another shop sells green tea, while ropes, pathways, and noticeboards keep the visitors in order. Nevertheless, Hōkokuji is one of the few of Kamakura's many temples to promote the study and practice of Zen among local residents. A popular zazenkai is held every Sunday morning from 8:00. Anyone is welcome, and participants include family groups with children. You do not have to notify the temple in advance of your attendance.

Newcomers are asked to arrive twenty to thirty minutes early for some basic instruction in the correct method of sitting. The temple will supply you with comfortable hakama. The meditation lasts about two hours, broken by spells of fast walking and even some running in a long line in the streets around the temple, as well as chanting of sutras and a sermon. Afterward, all participants receive a bowl of rice, and regulars engage in cleaning and maintenance of the temple, while newcomers introduce themselves at a special meeting. If you attend regularly you will learn of other activities, such as sesshin organized by members of the zazen-kai.

Foreigners sometimes attend, and a West German businessman, Jakob Blatte, felt sufficiently moved to write a book on his experiences at Hōkokuji, *The Diary of a Stranger in Japan* (Maruzen), in English, German, and Japanese, with many color photographs.

The meditation session is conducted strictly, but the atmosphere before and after is friendly and welcoming. It offers an interesting change from Sōtō practice, which seems to predominate among the English-language groups in Tokyo. The temple's location, however, makes it difficult to reach early on a Sunday morning for those not living nearby.

533 Jōmyōji, Kamakura-shi, Kanagawa-ken 248. Tel: (0467) 22-0762. A thirty-minute walk from Kamakura station, or a ten-minute bus ride. (But note that there are few buses early on Sunday morning.) It is marked on every tourist map of Kamakura.

報国寺　神奈川県鎌倉市浄明寺 533

INTERNATIONAL ZEN DŌJŌ　This is a small, Rinzai country temple, Seitaiji, set among trees and fields and surrounded by mountains, though little more than an hour's train journey from Tokyo. Some years ago the priest Sōtetsu Kanemaru began offering accommodation and instruction to Japanese people seriously interested in Zen. He speaks little English, but about seven years ago foreigners started arriving as well: he thinks the temple must have been mentioned in some foreign publications. Over the years more and more foreigners came—sometimes literally turning up on the doorstep—and so many people started calling the temple the International Zen Dōjō that Kanemaru Rōshi himself came to use the name. The temple is now listed with various tourist organizations as a place for Zen training, and Kanemaru Rōshi is sometimes telephoned by airport immigration officials or Foreign Ministry officers on behalf of a foreign arrival who is asking to study Japanese Zen.

Kanemaru Rōshi stresses that his temple is not a hotel. He wants only serious people who must be prepared to stay at least a week. He will not charge those who cannot pay. He describes his training as *kibishii*—strict. Students must get up early for zazen, and he uses the keisaku stick regularly to stimulate concentration. They will also be expected to study and to put in a lot of work in the fields and gardens around the temple.

Kanemaru Rōshi teaches calligraphy to students, and is also an expert on Buddhist vegetarian cuisine; he once wrote a series of articles on that subject for a Japanese magazine, and has taught its preparation to some students. Much of the food eaten at the temple is grown and prepared at home, including perhaps the best *takuan* pickles you will ever eat.

As noted, some foreigners have just turned up at the temple without advance notice. It is preferable, though, as well as much more polite, to contact Kanemaru Rōshi several days in advance. If you telephone, have a Japanese friend talk for you or speak very slow, clear English. Beginners are welcome, with the proviso that a week of zazen for someone with no experience can be physically demanding.

611 Tsurushima, Uenoharachō, Kita Tsuru-gun, Yamanashi-ken 409–01. Tel: (05546) 2–3198. A twenty-minute walk from Uenohara station on the Chūō line.

国際禅道場　山梨県北都留郡上野原町鶴島 611 青苔寺内

KANŌZAN KOKUSAI ZEN DŌJŌ   This new Rinzai Zen dōjō was opened in the mountains of Chiba Prefecture, west of Tokyo, to help foreigners wishing to study and practice Zen in Japan (*kokusai* means "international"). Foreigners are still welcome, but few go, and the English-language pamphlet once provided is no longer available. Today the dōjō basically operates as a center for groups from companies and schools who spend several days undergoing intensive Zen training. A weekend sesshin is held early each month, and occasionally notices of this are placed in Tokyo's English-language newspapers.

942–8 Takura, Futtsu-shi, Chiba-ken 299–16. Tel: (0439) 37-3011. The nearest station is Sanukimachi on the Uchibō line.

鹿野山国際禅道場　千葉県富津市田倉 942–8

RYŌBŌKAI   The Japanese-language pamphlet of this Rinzai Zen training center makes clear its objectives: "The Ryōbōkai Youth Training Dōjō is a center for providing social education to young people who, while living together in an orderly Zen-like manner, discipline their characters, deepen their feelings of fellowship, and become sound citizens, through zazen, martial arts, tea ceremony, recreation, and outdoor activities." While it is aimed mainly at groups, individuals are welcome, though it is preferred that they speak some Japanese. Most people generally come for short periods only, sometimes just for the weekend. A few foreigners have trained there.

The daily program includes intensive zazen and training in various disciplines, including karate and calligraphy. Among the facilities are a large martials arts dōjō and a zendō, as well as several small tatami rooms. The free pamphlet gives further details, including a map.

573 Honnō, Mobara-shi, Chiba-ken 299–41. Tel: (0475) 34-2355. A seven-minute walk from Honnō station on the Sotobō line.

両亡会　千葉県茂原市本納 573

Kyoto Area

Kyoto can perhaps best be described as the mecca of Japanese Buddhism. Here are found some of Japan's leading Zen temples and many of the head temples for the other sects. Some are national treasures which have strongly influenced Japanese culture. The city is the home of the seven great Rinzai monasteries: Daitokuji, Nanzenji, Tenryūji, Kenninji, Shōkokuji, Tōfukuji, and Myōshinji. All were founded in the thirteenth and fourteenth centuries, following the introduction of the Rinzai sect to Japan and the rise in Japan of the samurai class, who greatly favored the Zen tradition of Buddhism. In the following centuries these monasteries exercised enormous power over Japanese religious and cultural life. As a result, they are today major storehouses of Japanese art, much of which is on display to the public. Most of them also boast numerous subtemples within their own grounds, as well as branch temples throughout Japan.

Today, most of the seven monasteries function in a variety of roles. They administer thousands of branch temples throughout Japan. They preserve, restore, and guard the cultural heritage of centuries past. They open themselves to the millions of tourists who descend on Kyoto each year, and, officially, they pass on the teachings of their sect to young trainee priests, who will then disperse to the branch temples.

It is this last point that can cause some controversy. Unlike Eiheiji and Sōjiji, the two major Sōtō training temples, the Kyoto Rinzai monasteries are reluctant to reveal many details of their training methods or how to enter the sōdō. It is necessary to become the disciple of a particular teacher, who will then make all the arrangements. However, some sources have suggested that one reason the monasteries are so hesitant to talk is because they are suffering from a severe shortage of trainee priests, and that one or two may even have none at all. This problem became public in a small way in 1982 when a large Japanese daily newspaper, the *Mainichi Shimbun,* wrote that Myōshinji was dismayed that about a quarter of its 3,430 branch temples had no incumbent priest because so few young men were willing to undergo the rigorous training required of a novitiate. The paper noted that Myōshinji trainee priests with university degrees must undergo three years of training to enter the priesthood. This included rising at 3:30 each morning, compulsory attendance at lectures, zazen, sutra study, and manual labor. They must also practice *takuhatsu* (ritual mendicancy), are not allowed to read newspapers or watch television, must go to bed by 9:30 every evening, and receive only the most frugal of meals. The report also noted that Myōshinji has no intention of relaxing these requirements.

Foreigners have trained at most of the Kyoto monastery sōdō. But if you wish to follow in their footsteps you will need to have trained in Zen extensively beforehand, should speak Japanese, and, as noted, will need a teacher who can make all the necessary arrangements.

However, the monasteries sometimes offer chances to Kyoto residents to study and practice Zen. There are several zazenkai and some irregularly scheduled lecture series, as well as a number of individual priests who are pleased to offer their services to those who wish to learn. Some zazenkai are listed here, but it is necessary to be in Kyoto for an extended period in order to find out what else is going on. This can be done through such organizations as the Tourist Information Center, the English-language dailies (of the four, the *Mainichi Daily News* prints one of its editions in Osaka, near Kyoto, and probably covers the events of the city best), or by talking to people you meet at other Buddhist-oriented activities. Locating these monasteries is easy: they are on most tourist maps, and are also sign-posted around the city.

The zazenkai at these famous temples generally follow the same format—up to an hour of Zen meditation, preceded or followed by a talk on Buddhism (in Japanese, unless otherwise indicated), often from a famous Zen master. Usually there is an opportunity to chat over tea and cookies with the other participants and the temple priests. There is sometimes an application fee for new members, plus a small fee each time you attend, or else one annual charge.

Check with the temple before you attend, because schedules often change. For instance, many take a break during mid-summer. And you should locate the exact site of the zazenkai before the time of the meeting because some of the temples are vast complexes with numerous subtemples spread over a wide area. If the zazenkai is early in the morning there may be no one around to guide you to the right place.

Anyone who is interested in Buddhism or Japanese culture should try to visit these zazenkai at least once to experience the ambience of a centuries-old center and to establish helpful contacts. Furthermore, participants sometimes gain access to parts of the temple normally off-limits to the general public.

Several other Rinzai Zen temples in the city are smaller, and train few young priests, but are just as famous, especially among tourists. Ryōanji is known throughout the world for its sixteenth-century stone and sand garden. Kinkakuji (the Golden Pavilion) and Ginkakuji (the Silver Pavilion) are also celebrated for their gardens and glamorous buildings. In addition, Kyoto is home to numerous smaller Zen temples, to many famous temples of other Buddhist sects, and to shrines, palaces, castles, and museums.

One of Japan's holiest mountains, Mount Hiei, heart of the Tendai sect, is on the outskirts of the city, while another, Mount Kōya, home of Shingon Buddhism, is south in Wakayama Prefecture. (The neighboring business cities of Osaka and Kobe also boast a few temples of interest, though in general they are quite overshadowed by the riches of Kyoto.)

Of course, it is not necessary to go to Kyoto if you are interested in the practice of Japanese Buddhism. Some people even advise against it, asserting that the city is nothing but a nostalgic relic of the past, an elaborately and expensively preserved museum for the benefit of tourists, and that the Buddhism taught there is similarly stultified.

Certainly, you need not visit famous temples to study Zen. As several masters have noted, you can practice Zen in your own home, and visiting exotic temples is often just a form of sightseeing. Nevertheless, for the reasons noted above, few foreigners interested in Japanese Buddhism will want to miss a visit to the city. It is one of the great cultural capitals of the world, it boasts a long and vivid history, and it is home to many of the great Zen masters alive today.

A foreigner studying Buddhism here does not have to become attached to a single temple, but can instead study at many different centers. You will quickly meet other foreigners or English-speaking Japanese who will direct you to other places. You will also undoubtedly learn of priests who have visited foreign temples and Zen centers and who are sympathetic to Westerners wishing to practice in Kyoto. In addition, because Kyoto is the center for many traditional Japanese arts, especially those strongly connected with Buddhism such as the tea ceremony, you can spend time studying these.

Nevertheless, despite the variety of temples, Kyoto is not an easy place for the Westerner who does not speak Japanese and who has done little meditation before. An American man who has practiced Zen in Kyoto for many years comments: "The style here is mostly Rinzai, and to be honest it is not easy to get introductions to some of the temples. It is not as easy as you would expect it to be, considering that these are religious institutions. People sometimes get put off. You often need a lot of persistence and patience, especially when you don't speak much Japanese.

"Antaiji used to be the most important place for foreigners in Kyoto, but it later moved to Hyōgo Prefecture. Uchiyama Rōshi was in charge, and he welcomed foreign students of Zen. There were generally around twenty foreigners studying there at any one time. Now there are few priests like him who are prepared to sit down and help foreigners with their special problems. Nevertheless, I notice that foreigners in Kyoto nowadays are more serious than when I first arrived. In the 1960s the hippy culture was going strong, and a lot of people came here as part of some vague Asian pilgrimage. There were sometimes problems with drugs."

A further complicating factor is that some English-speaking priests and a few Westerners with particularly intimate experiences of Zen in Kyoto specifically requested that they not be named in this guide, for fear of a deluge of letters and phone calls. ("My name appeared in a foreign newspaper article," said one of these Japanese priests. "I started getting all kinds of strange letters. A lot of people expected me to solve their personal problems.") They are happy to help, but you will have to seek them out for yourselves. One excellent source of information is the Kyoto Tourist Information Center (TIC). The staff there are exceedingly friendly and keep up-to-date information on Zen temples suitable for foreigners.

But note the comments of one of the TIC's staff members: "Too many foreigners nowadays have the idea of taking a month's vacation from their jobs and coming to Kyoto for intensive Zen practice. They arrive at our office and expect us to direct them to some beautiful temple. They don't realize how strict the training can be here. It's not a holiday. And most of them haven't done any zazen before, so after a couple of days their legs and back are aching. We try to send visitors to a Zen group that fits their needs and experience, so we may direct a beginner to a morning zazenkai and a person with experience to one of various sesshin in the city. But when a person with no experience arrives and demands to be sent to some monastery for full-time training we have great difficulty helping him. There are now Zen groups all around the world. Such people should join one of those first to gain some experience before they arrive in Kyoto."

While no longer centers of practice, the ancient temples of nearby Nara, too, are well worth a visit. Because of the great distances involved, a sightseeing bus is the best way to take in Tōdaiji, Kōfukuji, Yakushiji, Hōryūji, Tōshōdaiji, and Jikōin. Not all tours stop at the last two temples so make sure the course you select includes them. Check with the TIC for details.

The TIC's address is Kyoto Tower Building, Higashi Shiokōji-chō, Shimogyō-ku, Kyoto 600. Tel: (075) 371–5649. It is opposite Kyoto station and right under Kyoto Tower.

ツーリスト・インフォーメィション・センター　京都市下京区東塩小路町 京都タワービル

DAITOKUJI   This great temple has had an enormous influence on Japanese religion and culture, and some refer to it as the most important Zen temple in the country. Volumes have been written on the temple's rich heritage. It was founded in 1319 and for many centuries counted both emperors and military leaders among its supporters. It attracted many of the country's most famous priests, who were often also great artists. Today it is still an impressive complex with many fine old buildings. Its massive gates and the central temple structures date from the sixteenth and seventeenth centuries, and some are designated national treasures. Over a dozen gardens are scattered throughout the temple, including some of the most famous in the country. Of the twenty-three subtemples, half-a-dozen are open to the public.

The garden at Daisen'in subtemple is 470 years old, and is renowned throughout Japan. It consists of a grouping of rocks, small trees, and gravel, and though occupying only a tiny space, it powerfully depicts a Chinese landscape painting. The Kōtōin subtemple boasts two famous tea houses, next to one of which stands a washbasin shaped from a stone brought to Japan from the imperial palace in Korea. This subtemple possesses several important paintings and other art objects, and the garden is particularly beautiful in autumn, when the maple trees display their rich colors.

The Ryōgen'in subtemple features not one but five gardens, including one that is said to be the smallest in Japan, and another that is thought to be the oldest in Daitokuji. Other treasures include some beautiful painted sliding doors and the oldest gun in Japan.

But Daitokuji, unlike some of the other temples of Kyoto, is far from being just a huge museum of Japanese culture. It is a living monastery, continually passing down the Zen teachings accumulated over hundreds of years. The monastery is also known for efforts made in the past to pass on its teachings to Westerners. Much of this came about through the work of Ruth Fuller Sasaki, an American who trained in Buddhism at the Nanzenji monastery and who in 1958 became abbot of Ryōsen'an, a subtemple of Daitokuji. She encouraged many Westerners in their study of Zen, and supervised the translation into English of some major Buddhist writings. She died in 1967, and today her temple is headed by a priest from Tokyo who, according to one source "speaks no English and seems to dislike foreigners." (But early morning zazen has been offered there for foreigners for several years. An invitation is necessary.)

Many foreigners have studied Zen at another of the monastery's subtemples, Ryōkōin, and the abbot of this temple speaks English. Some of the other subtemples offer various kinds of zazen, without regular schedules, and you will quickly learn of these if you spend some time in Kyoto. Daisen'in once offered a monthly zazenkai, but applications were required ten days in advance. Some Westerners have trained in the sōdō, including John Toler, an American, who is now head of Shōgen'in, a branch temple of Daitokuji in Nara Prefecture (p. 46).

Daitokuji is at 53 Daitokujichō, Murasakino, Kita-ku, Kyoto 603. Tel: (075) 491–0543.

大徳寺　京都市北区紫野大徳寺町 53

MYŌSHINJI　　Although founded in 1337, Myōshinji is unusual among the seven great Rinzai monasteries in that it did not achieve great political power for several centuries. During the late sixteenth century it came to be patronized by the warrior classes, and many of its subtemples owed their origin to samurai patrons. Perhaps because of its location on the outskirts of the city it is today the largest of the monasteries, with forty-seven subtemples dotted over the vast compound. Although it is near Ryōanji, it attracts relatively few tourists, and the spacious grounds are a favorite place for children playing baseball, old men taking a stroll, and young couples sitting under trees.

As noted, it boasts some 3,430 branch temples throughout the country, more than all other Rinzai monasteries put together. The temple bell, cast in 698, is the oldest in Japan, and is designated a national treasure. The temple is also rich in paintings and contains several famous gardens, but unfortunately few of these are on view to the public. One of the few subtemples you can visit without special permission is Taizōin. The garden there is thought by many to have been designed in the sixteenth century by the famous painter Kanō Motonobu. Many see in this garden—with its rocks, trees, bamboo grove, pond, and bridge—a landscape painting brought to life.

Myōshinji offers a zazenkai every weekend from Saturday 5:30 P.M. to Sunday 9:00 A.M., organized by the Myōshinji Zen Education Center.

Myōshinji is at 64 Myōshinjichō, Hanazono, Ukyō-ku, Kyoto 616. Tel: (075) 463–3121.

妙心寺　京都市右京区花園妙心寺町 64

NANZENJI　　Situated in a pine grove near the famous Heian Shrine, Nanzenji was founded in 1293. Before its establishment it was a detached palace of the emperor. Some of the present structures date back to the seventeenth century, including the main gate (*sammon*), which was built in 1628 and is decorated with pictures of celestial beings and birds. In the abbot's quarters are some renowned sliding screens, decorated by paintings entitled *Tigers in a Grove*. The seventeenth-century landscape garden is one of the most celebrated in the city. But many visitors come just for the delicious shōjin ryōri dishes served at two of Nanzenji's subtemples.

A regular zazenkai consisting of zazen only is held in the Nanzen'in subtemple, near the Main Hall, on the second and fourth Sundays of the month from 6:30 to 7:30 A.M. Short sesshin are sometimes arranged for special groups, and the monastery trains priests, though a temple administrator commented that this training was "not suitable for foreigners."

Fukuchichō, Nanzenji, Sakyō-ku, Kyoto 606. Tel: (075) 771–0365.

南禅寺　京都市左京区南禅寺福地町

TŌFUKUJI　　Founded in 1236, Tōfukuji is one of the oldest Zen temples in the city, and is still a vast complex, now split by numerous public streets running through the compound. But today it is not as rich in art treasures, gardens, or architectural masterpieces as some of the other monasteries, and it attracts fewer visitors. Perhaps this is also due to its location, southeast of Kyoto station, when most of the city's main sights are in the north.

The huge wooden entrance gate was built in the thirteenth century. The temple also holds some famous paintings, including works by the noted artist Sesshū. The gardens were redesigned in this century. They are especially popular in autumn for the rich colors of the maple trees. There is no regularly scheduled zazenkai for the general public. But one of the priests, Keidō Fukushima Rōshi, speaks excellent English and has several foreign disciples. He has also helped groups from abroad who wished to study and practice Zen in Japan, and is reported to be interested in having foreign monks come and live at Tōfukuji.

15 Hommachi, Higashiyama-ku, Kyoto 605. Tel: (075) 561–4632.

東福寺　京都市東山区本町 15

SHŌKOKUJI　Shōkokuji is smaller today than most of the other major Rinzai monasteries. It boasts comparatively few treasures, and is often missing from guidebooks. But for several centuries from the time of its foundation in 1392 it exerted considerable influence on court politics, with the chief priests frequently acting as advisors to the shoguns, rulers of Japan. Most of the buildings and many of the treasures were destroyed by the fires that ravaged the temple several times over the centuries.

The FAS ("Formless Awakened Self") Society, which was established by the well-known Zen scholar, the late Shin'ichi Hisamatsu, has recently moved its headquarters from Myōshinji to Shōkokuji, and sponsors a zazenkai there every Saturday from 4:00 to 8:00 P.M. When this meeting was held at Myōshinji it attracted many foreigners, and the proceedings were generally translated into English for them. It remains to be seen whether a similar pattern will develop at its new home. Another zazenkai, organized by the temple authorities, is held on the second and fourth Sunday of each month, from 9:00 to 11:00 A.M. Foreigners have trained in the sōdō.

Karasuma Higashi Iru, Imadegawa, Kamigyō-ku, Kyoto 602. Tel: (075) 231–0301; the FAS Society, (075) 811–9356.

相国寺　京都市上京区今出川烏丸東入ル

KENNINJI   Eisai, one of the founders of Rinzai Zen in Japan, established Kenninji on his return from a period of study in China, and hence it is often referred to as the cradle of Rinzai Zen. It is the oldest Zen temple in Kyoto. Kenninji is no longer open to the general public except with special permission, and then only in the morning. A zazenkai with a large attendance, generally including some foreigners, is held in the Kaisandō hall on the second Sunday of every month, from 8:00 to 10:00 A.M. Reservations are not necessary, and English-speaking people will often be around to give advice. A three-day training session (early mornings only) is scheduled every July. Foreigners have trained in the sōdō.

    584 Komatsuchō, Higashiyama-ku, Kyoto 584. Tel: (075) 561–0190.

    建仁寺　京都市東山区小松町 584

TENRYŪJI   This temple was founded in 1339, having formerly been a villa of the emperor Godaigo. At one time it extended over four square miles and boasted some 150 subtemples. All these have since been destroyed by the many fires which attacked the site over the years. The present buildings date from around the turn of this century. The main attraction today is the large garden, designed in the fourteenth century by the priest Musō Kokushi, regarded as one of Japan's great garden architects. The pond is in the shape of the Chinese character *kokoro,* meaning "heart," and is dotted with ancient rocks. On the far side of this pond is a dry waterfall, and the garden is thought to be one of the first in Japan to have incorporated "borrowed scenery"—natural external features which blend with the garden itself to create a pleasing effect. The borrowed scenery here includes two mountains, Arashiyama and Kameyama, which can be viewed as an extension of the garden.

    A Western priest has lived at a subtemple for some years, and foreigners have trained in the monastery, but there are no special provisions here for non-Japanese. Nor is there a zazenkai any longer. However, Seihō Hirata Rōshi, head of the monastery, speaks excellent German and some English, and Americans and Europeans have been welcomed at the temple.

68 Susukinobabachō, Saga Tenryūji, Ukyō-ku, Kyoto 616. Tel: (075) 881–1235.

天竜寺　京都市右京区嵯峨天竜寺芒ノ馬場町 68

SEITAIAN   Recently Seitaian has begun offering instruction in Zen in English, with beginners particularly welcomed. These are on the first and fourth Saturday of every month from 1:00 to 3:00 P.M. The teacher is Tom Wright, an American-born Sōtō Zen priest who is a long-time disciple of the noted master, Kōshō Uchiyama. A monthly five-day sesshin, sometimes attended by foreigners, is also held at this temple, but reservations by postcard are necessary, and there are no accommodations: you must find your own place to stay and commute every morning and evening. Only Japanese is spoken, and it starts on the Friday before the second Sunday of the month.

Gentaku Kitamachi, Ōmiya, Kita-ku, Kyoto 603. Tel: (075) 491–2579. Near Kitayama-dōri, northeast of Kinkakuji.

清泰庵　京都市北区大宮玄琢北町

RYŌANJI   World-famous for its abstract sand and stone garden, Ryōanji is thought to have been built in the early sixteenth century. Many people have tried to infer some meaning from the raked white sand and the fifteen rocks. Some say they represent a tiger with her cubs, while others see them as islands in the sea. The temple's own English-language brochure states that the garden is so profoundly meaningful that rather than make comparisons with other objects of this world it would be better to call it the "Garden of Nothingness," and the abbot of Ryōanji advises visitors to sit down quietly and contemplate.

Unfortunately, this is scarcely possible, as every day brings fresh busloads of foreign and Japanese tourists, while loudspeakers surrounding the garden blare out the history of the temple and garden. Quieter places are away from the garden, around the large lake, and in some of Ryōanji's subtemples. Regular zazenkai are scheduled at these, though an introduction is generally needed to attend. Many foreigners have participated and have highly acclaimed the instruction given by the presiding master. Once you have spent some time in Kyoto you will learn of the temple's activities.

Goryōnoshitachō, Ryōanji, Ukyō-ku, Kyoto 616. (075) 463–2216. A fifteen-minute walk from Ryōanji station on the Keifuku Electric Railway Kitano line. Marked on every tourist map.

竜安寺　京都市右京区竜安寺御陵ノ下町

SŌSENJI   This small, little-known Sōtō temple, is of no interest to the general tourist. But its highly popular Saturday zazenkai attracts foreigners because it is conducted by Kōshō Uchiyama Rōshi, who was particularly concerned with helping Westerners when he headed Antaiji before it moved from Kyoto to the mountains of Hyōgo Prefecture. He has had many foreign disciples. The zazenkai (which is conducted in Japanese) is at 2:00 P.M. on the third Saturday of the month. Another zazenkai, without Uchiyama Rōshi, is offered at Sōsenji on the first and third Mondays at 7:00 P.M.

Gojō Sagaru, Takakura-dōri, Shimogyō-ku, Kyoto 600. Tel: (075) 351–4270. Near Gojō station of the subway line.

宗仙寺　京都市下京区高倉通五条下ル

INSTITUTE FOR ZEN STUDIES   The Institute for Zen Studies (Zen Bunka Kenkyūjo) is a Rinzai-supported research body on the campus of Hanazono University (another Rinzai institution) that receives much of its financing from the tourist revenues at such popular temples as Ryōanji, Ginkakuji, and Kinkakuji. In recent years it has taken on a new role: providing assistance in English for the large numbers of Westerners who arrive in Kyoto in search of Zen practice and study. As such, it is an excellent source for information on temples and Zen groups in the city, and the staff will try to find an appropriate place to suit your experience.

The institute has published a short booklet in English which lists several Kyoto zazenkai suitable for foreigners and also contains preparatory exercises for those new to Zen meditation, the correct method of sitting, a Zen vocabulary list, and a short bibliography of books in English. It has also organized several intensive training sessions that gave foreigners the chance to live in a temple and receive instruction in English, and has helped many groups visiting the city to acquire a practical introduction to Zen.

The institute's excellent library includes books in English and is regularly consulted by scholars. It also organizes a weekly zazenkai, each Friday from 5:00 to 8:00 P.M. There is a token fee for tea and cakes. Bring your own teacup.

Hanazono University, 8–1 Tsubonouchichō, Nishinokyō, Nakagyō-ku, Kyoto 604. Tel: (075) 811–5189. A fifteen-minute walk from Hanazono station on the San'in line.

禅文化研究所　京都市中京区西ノ京壺ノ内町 8–1 花園大学内

ACADEMIC INSTITUTES　The Eastern Buddhist Society, cofounded by D.T. Suzuki, publishes the scholarly journal *The Eastern Buddhist*. The society has no other regular functions, but it is a good place to make academic contacts. The society's office is on the campus of Ōtani University, which is at Kamifusachō, Koyama, Kita-ku, Kyoto 603. Tel: (075) 432–3134.

The recently established School of Far Eastern Studies offers researchers such facilities as a library, a meeting room, individual desks, typewriters, and a copy machine. The school, open to scholars of all nationalities, is located on the fourth floor of the

Italian Cultural Center, 4 Ushinomiyachō, Yoshida, Sakyō-ku, Kyoto 606. Tel: (075) 751–1868. The Italian Cultural Center is near Kyoto University.

The International Association of Shin Buddhist Studies is active in translation work and occasionally sponsors English-language seminars. The association is on the campus of Ryūkoku University, 125–1 Daikuchō, Shichijō Agaru, Inokuma-dōri, Shimogyō-ku, Kyoto 600. Tel: (075) 343–3311.

Hongwanji International Center conducts Buddhist services in English, publishes a variety of translations, and maintains a seminary to train priests (Japanese and foreign) for overseas duty. The center is within the Nishi Hongwanji complex, Gakurinchō, Rokujō Sagaru, Higashi Nakasuji, Shimogyō-ku, Kyoto 600. Tel: (075) 371–5547.

東方仏教協会　京都市北区小山上総町　大谷大学内
イタリア文化センター　京都市左京区吉田牛ノ宮町 4
国際真宗学会　京都市下京区猪熊通七条上ル大工町 125–1 竜谷大学内
本願寺国際センター　京都市下京区東中筋六条下ル学林町　西本願寺内

SAIHŌJI   There is good news and bad news about Saihōji, the famous moss temple. The good news is that it is now open once a week to visitors, after being closed for several years because of damage to the celebrated garden, and that the conducted tour includes a short Zen Buddhist service. The bad news is that the price of admission is high and the Zen service, though genuine, is short and is clearly performed with tourists in mind. But this is the only way the general public can view the moss garden, and for many it may be a unique opportunity to join Zen priests in chanting the sutras of a Buddhist prayer service. If the fee of at least three thousand yen per person is no object, it is worthwhile.

Saihōji, a Rinzai temple, has its origins in the eighth century, though the foundation date is generally given as 1339, when the priest Musō Kokushi carried out a major reconstruction. He strongly believed that a garden was a vital aid for meditation. The garden at Saihōji spreads over 4½ acres, larger than many other temples, and is a wooded area covered with some forty varieties of green and yellow mosses. Tracks wind through the garden past the ancient Shonantei tea house (a national treasure), and around a pond which contains several moss-covered islands. The garden is at its finest in the spring, especially after a rain shower, when the whole effect can be quite stunning.

The general public can now visit only on Sunday afternoon, with advance application by return postcard necessary, stating name, address, age, and occupation. These are accepted up to three months before, on a first-come, first-served basis and must be received at least five days in advance. However, the temple tries to save a few places for short-term foreign tourists, and if you phone a day or two before (in Japanese) you will probably be accepted.

Visitors assemble at the front gate at 2:00 P.M. and a priest will take you on a short tour of the main buildings, then escort you to one of the halls for a lecture (in Japanese) on the history of the temple and the short service. This is an abbreviated version—about ten minutes long—of the morning services conducted at Zen monasteries throughout Japan, which often last up to one hour. A young priest chimes a gong, some others beat drums, and the oldest priest present says some short prayers, before leading everyone in sutra chanting (sutra sheets in Japanese are given to all visitors). Then you are asked to sit cross-legged for several minutes of zazen. But no instruction is given, and even many of the Japanese visitors are unsure of the correct posture. Finally, you are free to spend about forty minutes wandering around the garden. A map and short English-language guidebook are given to foreign visitors.

56 Jingatanichō, Matsuo, Nishikyō-ku, Kyoto 615. Tel: (075) 391–3631. A ten-minute walk from Matsuo station on the Hankyū Railway Arashiyama line.

西芳寺　京都市西京区松尾神ヶ谷町 56

MAMPUKUJI   Mampukuji is the head temple of the Ōbaku sect of Zen, which was transmitted from China in the seventeenth century. The temple was founded in 1661 by Ingen, a famous Ming-dynasty Chinese priest, and was modeled on Chinese temple buildings. The Main Hall, Daiyūhōden, was built of teak wood imported from Thailand.

Mampukuji incorporates what is known in English as the Young Men's Culture Training Center, which sponsors martial arts, cultural activities, and Zen-related activities. There is a sesshin from the first to the fifth of each month. All are welcome, men and women, and foreigners regularly attend. Participants are normally expected to arrive at the temple the night before the sesshin begins, for instruction in eating, bowing, and other etiquette. Only Japanese is spoken, but an English-speaking priest will normally be available to help foreigners, and this sesshin is recommended for those with little knowledge of Japanese. There is also a zazenkai from 2:00 to 5:00 P.M. on the first Sunday of the month.

The training center includes living facilities, and those who wish to study seriously at Mampukuji can enter after consultations with Gemmyō Murase, director of the center. Many foreigners have lived there, for periods of up to a year, doing regular zazen, receiving instruction from the head priest, and carrying out work in the temple grounds. The best time to inquire about this is at the end of a sesshin, when some participants often ask to stay on for further training. It is even possible to enter the sōdō after attending sesshin for up to a year, though no foreigners have taken this step.

Sambanwari, Gokanoshō, Uji-shi, Kyoto-fu 611. Tel: (0774) 32–3900. A five-minute walk from either the Ōbaku station on the Japan National Railways Nara line or the station of the same name on the Keihan Electric Railway Uji line.

万福寺　京都府宇治市五ヶ庄三番割

MOUNT HIEI   Although rather touristy in spots, much of

Mount Hiei, the headquarters of the Tendai sect, is unspoiled, despite its proximity to Kyoto; when walking along the mountain paths from temple to temple in the morning mist during early spring or late autumn it is not difficult to imagine yourself on a sacred peak. Often referred to as the fountainhead of Japanese Buddhism because so many founders of other sects first trained here, the Enryakuji monastery complex has a large number of stately temples and quite a few places of note. More important, however, is that it still maintains a solid tradition of practice. Unlike other monasteries where the majority are masquerading as monks, head priests on Mount Hiei voluntarily go through demanding training. Time must be spent in one of the "hells"— the sweeping hell at Jōdoin, the chanting hell at Yokawa, or the walking hells of Mudōji or Imuro valleys. One must also engage in practices such as standing under ice-cold waterfalls, performing thousands of daily prostrations, and completing ninety consecutive days of meditation. Interestingly, there are currently more candidates than ever.

The most famous practice associated with Mount Hiei is *sennichi kaihōgyō,* the thousand-day pilgrimage. Carried out in ten one-hundred-day terms over a seven-year period, it is the ultimate in walking meditation—eight terms of *daily* thirty to forty-kilometer (depending on the course) pilgrimages, one term of daily sixty-kilometer pilgrimages, and one incredible term of daily eighty-four-kilometer pilgrimages. There is also a special death-defying nine-day period of no eating, no drinking, no lying down, and no sleeping. The *gyōja,* as the pilgrims are called, may occasionally be seen striding briskly through Kyoto. A few foreigners have walked over the route informally in the "off season."

There are no regular programs for foreigners on Mount Hiei, but once in a while there are English-language sessions held at Kojirin, the Lay People's Training Hall, and it is also possible to stay at the Hall for a few days on an individual basis. The practice includes meditation (called *zazen shikan* in Tendai), jogging, *samu* (physical labor), sutra copying, study, and short mountain pilgrimages. One of the directors of Kojirin reportedly speaks English.

The Buddhist English Academy in Tokyo has occasionally arranged trips to Mount Hiei for study and practice, with instruction in English. And the Rev. Ichishima (leader of the Zen'yōji seminars, p.10), a Tendai priest, has arranged longer stays there for some foreigners, including his own disciples who were engaged in full-time study.

Kojirin, Hieizan, Sakamoto Hommachi, Ōtsu-shi, Shiga-ken 520–01. Tel: (0775) 78–0314. Mount Hiei is on every tourist map of the Kyoto region. There are various routes up the mountain, including buses and cable cars. These vary according to the season. Check at the Kyoto Tourist Information Center for up-to-date information.

居士林　滋賀県大津市坂本本町　比叡山

SANSHŌJI　　This is a small Sōtō Zen country temple set amidst rice paddies on the outskirts of Nara City that offers local residents and others a varied cultural program, including Zen meditation. There are regular courses in kendō, karate, aikidō, tea ceremony, ikebana, calligraphy, and Chinese poetry reciting as well as lecture series in various aspects of religion and culture.

The temple has a history of 480 years, although most of the current buildings are modern. A zazenkai is held every Wednesday and Saturday evening from 7:00 to 9:00, with foreigners often attending. Large groups sometimes stay for intensive Zen training sessions, and one group of eighteen Westerners spent ten weeks at the temple in 1978.

679 Shichijōchō, Nara-shi, Nara-ken 630. Tel: (0742) 44–3333. A fifteen-minute walk from Kujō station on the Kintetsu line.

三松寺　奈良県奈良市七条町　679

SHŌGEN'IN　　Zen priest John Toler attracted international

publicity when he took charge of Shōgen'in, a newly restored Rinzai temple in the hills of Nara Prefecture. Articles about the American-born former advertising man appeared in publications in many countries, usually noting how rare it is for a Westerner to be given charge of a temple in Japan. Some articles included photographs of celebrities who have visited Shogen'in, such as former Prime Minister Takeo Fukuda, while *Life* magazine had a photo of Toler conducting a tea ceremony for a glamorous model as part of a feature on Japanese fashion.

The fifty-three-year-old Toler arrived in Japan in 1954 as a member of the U.S. armed forces and became one of many American military men who elected to stay in the country when their tour of duty was over. He later began working for an advertising company, and also started his study of Zen, which led to his entering Daitokuji in Kyoto for training as a priest. There he underwent long hours of meditation, interspersed with sutra chanting, study, and hard physical labor. He recalls that the trainee priests were often required to tramp the snow-covered streets of Kyoto on begging expeditions wearing only straw sandals. Another American who entered training with him found it all too much and escaped one night by climbing over the wall.

Shōgen'in was once a subtemple within the compound of Daitokuji, but it was closed down in the nineteenth century. Rebuilding began in 1979 at a 270-year-old manor house in the town of Ōuda, Nara Prefecture. Set in the hills and commanding magnificent views over rice paddies and small groves, it has twenty-seven rooms, including several especially designed for the tea ceremony. A famous garden architect was called in to construct the rock garden, and the main hall was erected according to traditional designs.

Neighborhood people sometimes arrive for morning zazen, conducted after Toler has rung the huge temple bell at 6:00 A.M., sending the chimes reverberating through the valleys. Japanese and foreigners have often stayed for several days at a time, by arrangement, but there is no fixed program. However, Toler is well aware that his training leaves him in a unique position to help others in the West who wish to learn about Zen, particularly those who speak no Japanese, and he is willing to share the fruits of his experiences with those who have a serious interest.

Ōudachō, Uda-gun, Nara-ken 633–21. Tel: (07458) 3–0384. A fifteen-minute taxi ride from Haibara station on the Kintetsu line.

松源院　奈良県宇陀郡大宇陀町

KAISEIJI　This Rinzai Zen training temple offers a Sunday zazenkai twice a month which is sometimes attended by foreigners. Several Westerners, including a few European Catholic priests, have also lived there for varying lengths of time, studying and practicing Zen with the priests. The zazenkai is on the first and third Sunday each month from about 8:00 A.M. All are welcome, including beginners, for whom some elementary instruction will usually be given. About two hours of zazen are followed by a lecture and a light lunch. Participants are expected to do samu around the temple before the zazenkai ends at around 1:00 P.M.

As noted, a few Westerners have lived at the temple for varying periods, but Kaiseiji is for serious lay students only, preferably those with experience in Zen and the ability to speak Japanese. There is no set procedure for arranging to practice there. If you attend the zazenkai regularly you can express a desire to participate in one of the six sesshin held each year (usually the first week of October, November, December, May, June, and July). After attending some sesshin it may be possible to arrange to stay for a longer time, perhaps six months to a year, living in one of the temple rooms separate from the trainee priests but practicing with them. Accommodation for lay people is limited, however, and seldom will more than one or two be allowed to stay at any time.

7–25 Rokutanjichō, Nishinomiya-shi, Hyōgo-ken 662. Tel: (0798) 22–2637. A short walk from Nishinomiya station.

海清寺　兵庫県西宮市六湛寺町 7–25

SHITENNŌJI   This huge Osaka temple is the headquarters of the small Washū Tendai sect, and is one of the major Buddhist institutions in Osaka. It was founded in 593, though most of the present buildings are modern constructions. It has recently renamed its junior college "The International Buddhist University," so perhaps it has some grand plans. To date these have not been revealed, though in 1983 the *Mainichi Daily News* reported that the university plans to build an Islamic mosque on the campus and to initiate courses in Arab language and culture, with the aim of promoting mutual understanding and student exchanges between Japan and Islamic countries. A university official told the newspaper that Buddhist students would be enriched by the opportunity to see students from Islamic countries offering prayers in the mosque.

The University sometimes sponsors both zazenkai and seminars on Buddhist history and culture open to the general public. Check with them for details.

The temple is at 1–11–18 Shitennōji, Tennōji-ku, Osaka 543. Tel: (06) 771–0066. It is near the Shitennōjimae station on the Tanimachi subway line. The University is at 1308 Hanyūno, Habikino-shi, Osaka-fu 583. Tel: (0729) 56–3181. A bus ride from Fujiidera station on the Kintetsu line.

四天王寺　大阪市天王寺区四天王寺 1–11–18

四天王寺国際仏教大学　大阪府羽曳野市植生野 1308

FUGENJI   The Japanese headquarters of the Korean Sōkei Zen sect has no special programs for foreigners, but can provide information on Korean Buddhism.

5–12–39 Katsuyama Kita, Ikuno-ku, Osaka 544. Tel: (06) 712–1015. Call in Japanese for directions.

普賢寺　大阪市生野区勝山北 5–12–39

JŌKŌIN   The Rev. Taikō Yamasaki, priest at this Shingon temple, teaches a regular class in esoteric Buddhism on the second

Sunday of each month, from 2:00 to 4:00 P.M. Anyone is welcome, and foreigners often attend (although everything is in Japanese). Each session includes a lecture, some yoga, and *ajikan* meditation, which involves meditating on a stylized Sanskrit letter set against a white disc and placed on an eight-petaled white lotus.

The Rev. Yamasaki has taught esoteric Buddhism to groups of foreigners who have come to Kyoto to study Japanese culture, and is working with students on a book in English on the subject.

1–3–3 Shinonome-dōri, Chūō-ku, Kobe-shi, Hyōgo-ken 651. Tel: (078) 221–3380. A fifteen-minute walk from Kasuganomichi station on the Hanshin line.

常光院 兵庫県神戸市中央区東雲通 1–3–3

SHŌFUKUJI   Foreigners have practiced regularly at this big Rinzai training temple in Kobe City, west of Kyoto, and the head abbot, Taitsu Kano, has visited the San Francisco Zen Center and has encouraged foreigners in their practice. Nevertheless, it is generally necessary to be able to communicate in Japanese, to have an introduction, and to have some experience in Zen in order to practice at Shōfukuji. There are seven one-week sesshin each year—in May, June, July, October, November, December, and January—and lay groups sit in the main hall during these, but in the evening only, without staying overnight. The temple can be contacted through the Institute for Zen Studies in Kyoto.

Gonomiyachō, Hyōgo-ku, Kobe-shi, Hyōgo-ken 652. Tel: (078) 361–0378. A ten-minute bus ride from Sannomiya station.

祥福寺 兵庫県神戸市兵庫区五宮町

MOUNT KŌYA   It is not easy to categorize Mount Kōya, the headquarters of the Shingon sect: is it a holy site to practice Tantric Buddhism in the presence of Kōbō Daishi, who resides there in eternal meditation? Or is it a center of pilgrimage and repentance for the devoted believer in the great saint? Or is the entire place one giant confidence game set up to fleece the weak and gullible?

Or is it a pleasant resort town with all the diversions any Japanese tourist could hope for? Incorporating a bizarre, exhilarating mixture of the sacred and the profane, the sublime and the hideous, transcendental wisdom and crude superstition, the charm of Mount Kōya is impossible to describe.

All of the temples are in the hotel business, catering to the busloads of "pilgrims" (1.3 million per year), who flood the mountain in summer and on other special days, so you have a choice of more than fifty temples for accommodations. At least a little English is spoken in many of them; prices for a one-night stay start from six thousand yen, but include two hearty and delicious Buddhist vegetarian meals. (The youth hostel, Henjōson'in, is cheaper.) If you go in the off-season (early spring and late autumn; winter is extremely cold) things are more peaceful. There is an English-language booklet available at the tourist reception center near Mount Kōya station.

The following places are the best to visit or stay at for foreigners interested in Buddhism.

Friendly and outgoing Haruki Shizuka, assistant head priest at Fukuchiin, the largest temple accommodations on the mountain, is an enthusiastic speaker of English and enjoys discussing Buddhism with foreigners. He is busy, so telephone or write before dropping in.

Both the head and the assistant head priest of Yōchiin speak English (they have a branch temple in the U.S.). They occasionally give instruction in Shingon practice, and a few foreigners have practiced here. For information contact Kōgi Aratano, the assistant head priest.

Shinnōin is administered by Head Priest Zenkyō Nakagawa, former president of Kōya University and the sole holdout on Kōya who does not eat meat or drink sakè and has not married. Nakagawa is reported to have an American disciple. He is now semiretired, so do not trouble him unless you have an introduction or make an appointment well in advance.

By the way, stop in and see Mr. Fumio Nishimoto, proprietor of Nishiri Art Gallery (near the central area). He says his German is better than his English—he vacations in Germany every year—but handles both well, and likes to chat about affairs, local and international.

There is some actual training done on Mount Kōya—a strictly run "Senshū Gakuin" for Shingon novices and one small "Precepts" temple—but such things are generally not taken seriously. The address for all Mount Kōya temples is Kōyasan, Kōyamachi, Ito-gun, Wakayama-ken 648.

It takes about two hours to reach Mount Kōya on the Kōyasan Railway line from the Nankai station in Osaka, followed by a five-minute cable-car ride and a short bus trip to the top of the mountain. Everything of note can be seen in a day, but an overnight stay is recommended to sample the food and attend the 6:30 morning service held at every shukubō.

The telephone numbers of the four temples are: Henjōson'in, home of Mount Kōya youth hostel, (07365) 6–2434; Fukuchiin, (07365) 6–2021; Yōchiin, (07365) 6–2003; Shinnōin, (07365) 6–2227.

遍照尊院・福智院・桜池院・親王院　和歌山県伊都郡高野町高野山

KAIŌJI   This is one of the few temples in Japan where foreigners are made welcome at any time for Zen instruction. It is a small Rinzai temple with a relaxed atmosphere. The priest in charge, Sōsen Takeuchi, speaks a little English. He has also prepared an English-language pamphlet with basic Zen instruction. Kaiōji is highly recommended, especially for those with little or no Zen experience. Katsuura is a well-known hot-springs resort town in Wakayama Prefecture, about four hours by train from either Nagoya station or Tennōji station in Osaka. The temple, which is on a hill overlooking a very pretty bay, is registered as a youth hostel, and it is even possible to stay without participating in morning zazen.

Many foreigners have visited, and the visitors' book is full of glowing comments on the hospitality of the priest and his family (as well as, sometimes, more succinct remarks on the agony of several days of zazen). Among the added attractions are Buddhist vegetarian dishes cooked by the priest's wife and instruction in sumi-e ink painting, calligraphy, and tea ceremony. The temple boasts its own small zendō, and regular sesshin are held there. These are scheduled for February 10–15, April 1–7, June 1–7, August 1–7, October 7–12, December 1–8, and December 31–January 1. Three of these—April, August, and the end-of-year sesshin—are for women only.

Participants in the sesshin normally sleep in the zendō itself. Other guests can be accommodated in one of several spare rooms in the main temple building. Reservations are necessary for both sesshin and other stays. If you hope for some intensive training at a time other than a sesshin you should consult first with Takeuchi Rōshi.

642 Katsuura, Nachi Katsuurachō, Higashi Muro-gun, Wakayama-ken 649–53. Tel: (07355) 2–0839. A ten-minute walk from Katsuura station.

海翁寺　和歌山県東牟婁郡那智勝浦町勝浦 642

Other Areas

Nearly every area has at least one temple that offers zazen or some other kind of Buddhist training, and if you ask around you will find it. Often it is in the most remote places that the most wonderful manifestations of innen occur. While you cannot expect English at many of these places, there are unlikely to be restrictions on sincere foreigners, and at some you may find yourself welcomed most enthusiastically.

EIKYŌJI INSTITUTE OF ZEN STUDIES   This recently established institute, a nonsectarian Buddhist study center, plans to open an international seminary within the next five years. Current activities center on scholarly research and publishing English-language books on Buddhism. The institute, run by two Japanese priests who were formerly American college professors, welcomes inquiries but asks that visitors make advance appointments.

Jun Takeda, Institute Secretary, 156 Tadoshichō, Fukagawa-shi, Hokkaidō 074–01. Tel: (01642) 7–2703 (in English, during business hours); (01642) 7–2702 (in Japanese). A 2½-hour drive from Sapporo.

永教寺　北海道深川市多度志町 156

CHŪŌJI   In Sapporo one can do zazen at Chūōji, a large Sōtō temple in the heart of the city. There is a zazenkai every Sunday morning from 9:00 (9:30 in winter) and it is possible to attend the early morning zazen (from 4:45) if you request permission. However, there are no facilities for overnight accommodation.

Nishi 2-chome, Minami Rokujō, Chūō-ku, Sapporo-shi, Hokkaidō 053. Tel: (011) 512–7321. Chūōji is centrally located, near Sapporo station.

中央寺　北海道札幌市中央区南六条西 2 丁目

OSOREZAN ENTSŪJI   Japanese Buddhism is not all monks doing zazen; for a glimpse at the "other side of the circle" visit Osorezan if you happen to be in this remote area of northern Japan. Osorezan, "Dreadful Mountain," is a volcanic area on the Shimokita Peninsula, Aomori Prefecture, full of sulfur hot springs bubbling from the rocks and blood-red pools of scalding water. As a *reijo,* a place where departed souls linger, it is a point of contact between this world and the next. Twice a year, from July 20 to 24 and in the first week of September, Entsūji, a Sōtō temple, sponsors a festival in which *itako,* blind female mediums, make contact with the dead and predict the future for parishioners and other petitioners. The prophecies of the itako are said to be uncannily accurate. Light-years away from the usual disciplined matter-of-factness of Zen, the goings-on at Osorezan represent the immemorial traditions of folk religion and shamanism. There is a shukubō attached to the temple but it caters to true pilgrims, so tourists should either camp on the eerie, semilunar landscape or stay elsewhere on the peninsula. Further information is available in *Exploring Tōhoku: A Guide to Japan's Back Country* by Jan Brown (John Weatherhill).

Osorezan Entsūji is located at 4–11 Shimmachi, Mutsu-shi, Aomori-ken 035. Tel: (01752) 2–1091.

恐山円通寺　青森県むつ市新町 4–11

DEWA SANZAN   Just a mention of the name Dewa Sanzan
(the three Dewa mountains—Mount Haguro, Mount Yudono,
and Mount Gassan) is enough to send chills running down the
spines of many Japanese. This isolated region of northern Japan is
the home of a branch of the *yamabushi,* an ancient order of mountain ascetics who continue a twelve-hundred-year religious tradition that combines Buddhism, Shintōism, Taoism, primitive
mountain worship, mysticism, folk religion, and shamanism. The
weather on these rugged mountains is so fierce that the ski season
cannot begin before April and lasts until August. During winter,
parts of the mountains are inaccessible, though this does not stop
the yamabushi, who schedule some of their most important rituals
for this period. The haiku poet Bashō visited Dewa Sanzan in the
late seventeenth century during his journey to the deep north of
Japan. He said that the rules he had to obey as a pilgrim precluded
him from detailing the wonders he saw on the mountains. But
of Mount Haguro, he wrote that "the awe-inspiring majesty of
this sacred peak will never fade."

One of the more eerie features of the yamabushi cult was the
now outlawed practice of self-mummification. Certain ascetics
felt that by "becoming Buddha in this very body" society would
benefit—the merit of one Buddha would be transferred to all
sentient beings. This involved a ten-year ritual designed to get rid
of virtually all body fat, to wither the body, and to rot the internal
organs. The first forty months saw the ascetic (they were generally
not priests, but ordinary lay believers) cut out his intake of all
cereal crops. For the second forty months he ate nothing but fruits,
berries, and plant roots. At the end of this period he was virtually
a living mummy, little more than a skin-covered skeleton. He then
entered a small underground room which was covered with earth.
He breathed through a bamboo pipe extending above ground,
chanted sutras, and awaited death. After a final forty months the
covering of earth was removed, and the mummified body was

enshrined in a temple. Some were found only recently, and it is presumed that others remain buried, awaiting discovery.

Although demanding, the austerities now undertaken by present-day yamabushi are less severe than in earlier days; still, few full-time practitioners remain. Most hold regular jobs (several, for example, work as bus drivers and train conductors) and the majority are married with families. Most of the Dewa Sanzan buildings are on Mount Haguro, which remains reasonably accessible in winter. At the foot of the mountain, just past a huge torii, or Shintō gateway, is a large collection of shukubō where pilgrims traditionally stay. A little further on is a spectacular, six-hundred-year-old pagoda, perhaps the most beautiful in Japan, and designated a national treasure. You can take a bus to the top of the mountain, but it is better to walk the 2,446 stone steps which wind between giant cedar trees. At the top is a collection of religious buildings and a history museum. Mount Haguro is popular with tourists, but the other two peaks attract mainly pilgrims, who climb to the top to worship at the shrines there—the 1,900-meters-high Gassan is considered especially holy.

For many centuries the shrines at the foot of Mount Haguro have offered accommodation to pilgrims. At one time there were one hundred or more of these places, but with the ease of transportation today's pilgrims often prefer to stay in one of the nearby hot spring resorts, and only about thirty shrines still take overnight guests. Prices are generally a little higher than at many shukubō, but the quality of accommodation is high, comparable to that at Mount Kōya, and you receive two delicious shōjin ryōri meals with your lodgings.

Miyatabō, a large old shrine, has had foreign guests (although no English is spoken). There are many large rooms, and the meals are excellent, incorporating the well-known *sansai* (wild vegetables) of the region. All visitors are expected to get up early to attend the stirring morning service, which includes one priest blowing the traditional yamabushi conch shell while others chant and tend a roaring fire.

Pilgrims generally come in their own groups, but non-profit groups affiliated with some of the shrines on the mountains also organize yamabushi training sessions which are open to the public. Unlike Zen training, where much of your time is spent in meditation, these programs stress physical activities. They include purification exercises under waterfalls, mountain climbing, and esoteric meditation. You must be able to speak some Japanese and be in good physical condition. A further drawback is that the mountains are difficult to reach. Most people come by bus from the nearby city of Tsuruoka. One program takes place every weekend (noon Friday to noon Sunday) during August, September, and October, organized by a group called Yamabushi Shugyō no Tabi. A second weekend program takes place twice each year, in July and August, run by another organization, Yudonosan Sanrōjo. Several Westerners have taken part in both programs.

You can also ask officials at both these centers about the week-long pilgrimage held on the mountain in late summer every year. This is not generally open to the public, though by attending one of the programs cited above you can discuss applying to join. Many of the Dewa Sanzan yamabushi take part in this pilgrimage, and religious ascetics and shamans from around Japan also attend. Participants spend much of their time in prayer and chanting sutras; they receive only minute quantities of food and drink, and are allowed little sleep. They pass through several symbolic stages, from dumb animalhood to death (attending their own "funeral service"), before attaining a symbolic enlightenment, which is celebrated with holy services on the peaks of the three mountains.

Reservations for shukubō on Mount Haguro can be made in Japanese through the Planning Department of the Haguromachi Office (Haguromachi Yakuba Kikakuka), Arakawa, Haguromachi, Higashitagawa-gun, Yamagata-ken 997. Tel: (0235) 62–2111. Miyatabō is at Tōge, Haguromachi, Higashitagawa-gun, Yamagata-ken 997. Tel: (0235) 62–2268. Yamabushi Shugyō no Tabi is at Yudonosan Tansei Shugyō Dōjō, Asahimura, Higashitagawa-gun, Yamagata-ken 997. Tel: (0235) 54–6131. Yudonosan Sanrōjo is at Asahimura, Higashitagawa-gun, Yamagata-ken 997. Tel: (0235) 54–6131.

羽黒町役場　山形県東田川郡羽黒町荒川
宮田坊　山形県東田川郡羽黒町手向
湯殿山丹生修業道場　山形県東田川郡朝日村
湯殿山参籠所　山形県東田川郡朝日村

ZEN ART SOCIETY   At present this society, headed by co-author John Stevens, offers no regular programs, but it is a good source of information on all aspects of Zen culture and Buddhist art.

1–37–2 Tsurugaya, Sendai-shi, Miyagi-ken 983. Tel: (0222) 51–5580.

禅美術研究会　宮城県仙台市鶴ヶ谷 1–37–2

RINNŌJI   This Sōtō temple, noted for its lovely garden, conducts a zazenkai every Saturday evening, from 6:00 to 8:00 (in Japanese only). There is a small charge to cover the cost of tea and cakes. Foreigners are welcome and regularly attend.

1–14–1 Kitayama, Sendai-shi, Miyagi-ken 980. Tel: (0222) 34–5327. The Sendai City Kitayama Shiheimachi bus line stops at the temple's front gate.

輪王寺　宮城県仙台市北山 1–14–1

ZUIGANJI   This well-known, beautifully constructed old Rinzai temple in the tourist spot of Matsushima, about thirty minutes from Sendai, occasionally permits serious foreigners to attend sesshin with the monks. A personal interview or letter of recommendation is necessary. Anyone may participate in the irregularly scheduled zazenkai. The three-hundred-year-old zendō has an especially nice "feel" to it.

91 Matsushimachō, Miyagi-gun, Miyagi-ken 981–02. Tel: (02235) 4–3038. A short walk from Matsushima Kaigan station on the Senseki line.

瑞巌寺　宮城県宮城郡松島町 91

EIHEIJI NAGOYA BETSUIN　This is another branch of Eiheiji, the Sōtō Zen *honzan,* or head temple. A zazenkai is held on the second and fourth Saturday each month, from 2:00 to 3:00 P.M.

41–32 Daikanchō, Higashi-ku, Nagoya-shi, Aichi-ken 461. Tel: (052) 936–2010. Four kilometers from Nagoya station.

永平寺名古屋別院　愛知県名古屋市東区代官町 41–32

EMMONJI　This temple sponsors a Sunday morning zazenkai that is organized and operated by lay men and women. Zazen is from 9:00 to 10:30. This is followed by an open discussion (in Japanese) and a cleaning of the premises. Foreigners are welcome to participate. A small fee is required.

2–53 Sugimurachō, Kita-ku, Nagoya-shi, Aichi-ken 462. Tel: (0528) 831–6720.

円文寺　愛知県名古屋市北区杉村町 2–53

TOKUGENJI　This Rinzai temple has zazen every Saturday from 6:00 to 8:00 P.M.; it includes a lecture on a Zen text by the head priest.

2–41 Shindeki, Higashi-ku, Nagoya-shi, Aichi-ken 461. Tel: (052) 936–2698. Five kilometers from Nagoya station.

徳源寺　愛知県名古屋市東区新出来 2–41

TŌGANJI　This temple has an interesting connection with India and Southeast Asia. Founded by the historic Oda clan, it has numerous Indian-style statues, including a Shiva lingam, and Head Priest Baisen Oda specializes in the study of early Buddhism. One of the monks there has studied in India, and several Sri Lankan priests have stayed at Tōganji. The temple has a tenuous relationship to the Sōtō organization. It is not open to the public, and no English is spoken, but Oda Sensei is a fount of information for scholar-practitioners who have an introduction or call in advance to arrange a visit.

2–16 Yotsuya-dōri, Chikusa-ku, Nagoya-shi, Aichi-ken 464. Tel: (052) 781–1427. A short walk from the Hon'yama subway station.

桃巌寺　愛知県名古屋市千種区四谷通 2–16

SHŌSŌJI　This is a small Sōtō temple in the countryside about forty minutes from the popular tourist city of Takayama. The priest, Dōichi Harada, speaks a little English and has traveled to such countries as India, Israel, and America (where he conducted a sesshin in Omaha, Nebraska). His widely divergent objects of admiration include the kibbutz system, Mahatma Gandhi, and samurai. He is happy to help anyone who is serious about practicing Zen, and, by arrangement, you can stay in his temple. It is a small place, and he cannot accommodate large groups. He says that ideally he would prefer just one person at a time. He also stresses that while he welcomes foreigners he will not make any special allowances for them—he treats everyone the same. Fees and length of stay are by consultation, though short visits are preferred. This is an excellent place for a person serious about Zen—even someone with little experience—who desires the opportunity of living for a short time in a Japanese country temple.

Kitakata, Nyūkawamura, Ōno-gun, Gifu-ken 506. Tel: (05777) 8–1080. A forty-minute bus ride from Takayama to Nyūkawa village.

正宗寺　岐阜県大野郡丹生川村北方

ZENTSŪJI　Zentsūji is an old Rinzai temple in the hot springs mountain resort of Shinhirayu, in central Japan. It is better known as Enkuan, in recognition of its famous collection of wooden Buddha statues carved by the seventeenth-century itinerant priest

Enku. A cheap *minshuku* (Japanese family inn) is in the temple precincts, boasting its own hot mineral water pool for guests.

There is daily zazen here for an hour from 5:00 A.M. In fact, notices around the temple insist that guests and others who wish to view the Enku statues must first do an hour's Zen meditation. You should give notice by 9:00 the previous evening of your intention to participate. The priest speaks a little English, and several Westerners have stayed there. Shinhirayu is surrounded by hiking tracks, and in winter there is skiing nearby.

Shinhirayu, Hitoegane, Kamitakaramura, Yoshiki-gun, Gifu-ken 506–14. Tel: (0578) 9–2106. A ninety-minute bus ride from Takayama.

禅通寺　岐阜県吉城郡上宝村一重ヶ根新平湯

ZENNŌJI   This is one of about a dozen temples at the foot of the line of hills in the Teramachi District on the outskirts of Taka-yama, a small city in central Japan often referred to as "Little Kyoto" for the traditional architecture of many of its buildings. Because of its beauty, the city attracts many tourists, particularly for the spectacular spring festival, in which excited residents drag two dozen decorated floats through the streets. But with a popula-tion of only some sixty thousand people, the city has little in the way of Buddhist practice. Only Zennōji offers regular zazen, from 6:00 to 7:00 A.M. each day. This depends on the season, however, and may not take place in winter. Each December there is a five-day sesshin.

The temple also organizes occasional two-day Zen seminars, with lectures on Buddhist history, culture, and practice (in Jap-anese), and intensive zazen. Foreigners have attended these, and are welcome again, although you are unlikely to encounter anyone who speaks English. But it is an excellent chance to see Takayama, an enchanting city. The temple is also listed in some guidebooks as being able to accommodate tourists, but this is subject to prior negotiation.

177 Sōyūjimachi, Takayama-shi, Gifu-ken 506. Tel: (0577) 32–4516. A fifteen-minute walk from Takayama station.

禅応寺　岐阜県高山市宗猷寺町 177

TSUBAKI GRAND SHRINE　Tsubaki Grand Shrine in central Japan recently began offering foreigners the chance to experience the ancient practices of Shintō, Japan's native religion, by joining in the daily life there. This includes a morning service and *misogi* purification rituals under a waterfall. Priest Yukitaka Yamamoto has also established an International Division in Tokyo, to provide information in English on Shintō, and hopes to open a shrine and cultural center in San Francisco.

Yamamotochō, Suzuka-shi, Mie-ken 519–03. Tel: (0593) 71–1515. For reservations, directions, and further information contact the International Division in Tokyo (in English): Mr. Shunkichi Inokuma, Hikawa Annex Building No. 2, Room 307, 6–9–5 Akasaka, Minato-ku, Tokyo 107. Tel: (03) 583–6637.

椿大神社　三重県鈴鹿市山本町

椿大神社東京講本部　港区赤坂 6–9–5 氷川アネックス 2 号館 307

DAIANJI　This very beautiful Rinzai Zen temple in the mountains surrounding Fukui City in central Japan was once the family temple of a branch of the Matsudaira clan, lords of the area, and still retains many treasures. The assistant priest, Yūhō Takahashi, has visited several Zen centers in America and welcomes foreigners to the regular Friday evening zazenkai.

21–4 Tanotanichō, Fukui-shi, Fukui-ken 910. Tel: (0776) 59–1014. A ten-minute taxi ride from Fukui station.

大安寺　福井県福井市田ノ谷町 21–4

EIHEIJI　Although Eiheiji is not especially recommended, most experienced practitioners and Sōtō Zen Buddhists will want to see this famous temple founded by Dōgen near the Japan Sea. Short-term visitors can stay a minimum of two nights and three days and a maximum of six nights and seven days. You are put in a special building for lay practitioners called Kichijōkaku, and join the monks only for the morning service (which is most impressive). The visitors' schedule parallels that for the trainee priests (in winter the schedule begins an hour later):

3:30 A.M.	Rise	11:30–2:00	Free time
3:45–5:30	Zazen	2:00–4:30	Zazen
5:30–7:00	Morning service in main hall	4:30–5:00	Evening service
		5:30–6:00	Dinner
7:00–7:30	Breakfast	6:00–7:10	Free time (bath, etc.)
7:30–10:00	Samu		
10:00–11:00	Zazen	7:10–8:30	Zazen
11:00–11:30	Lunch	9:00 P.M.	Lights out

The zazen periods are forty to forty-five minutes, broken by *kinhin,* five minutes or so of walking Zen.

Applications must be made at least ten days in advance by return postcard with name, address, telephone number, occupation, sex, age, proposed dates of stay, reason for your visit, and zazen experience (all in Japanese, of course). Eiheiji is closed to outsiders from January 1 to 13, February 8 to 15, April 20 to 30, July 12 to 18, August 10 to 20, September 20 to 30, and December 28 to 31.

Sanzenkai, Eiheiji, Eiheijichō, Yoshida-gun, Fukui-ken 910–12. Tel: (0776) 63–3102. A short walk from Eiheiji station on the Keifuku line.

永平寺　福井県吉田郡永平寺町

SHŌMYŌJI　An Ōbaku temple run by Ninpō Okuda Rōshi, who has held training sessions in Europe and the U.S., and works closely with the founder of Oki Yoga.

1 Matsuo, Hinochō, Gamō-gun, Shiga-ken 529–16. Tel: (07485) 2–0227. Four kilometers from Hino station on the Ōmi line.

正明寺　滋賀県蒲生郡日野町松尾 1

CHŌKOKUJI   This is not a training temple. The head priest
here, Hōryū Sahashi, is a well-known scholar and critic of con-
temporary Japanese Buddhism. He will discuss, in difficult Japanese, academic subjects with foreigners. Meetings must be
arranged in advance.

1015 Tamachi, Matsushiromachi, Nagano-shi, Nagano-ken
381–12. Tel: (0262) 78–2454. Five hundred meters from Matsu-
shiro station on the Nagano line.

長国寺　長野県長野市松代町田町 1015

DAIJŌJI   A lovely six-hundred-year-old Sōtō Zen temple in
Kanazawa, Daijōji has only a few monks training there at present.
It is possible to stay for a couple of days and join the practice,
which consists of a lot of heavy labor (samu). Arrangements must
be made in advance. Morning zazen from 4:30 to 5:30 is open to
all. The morning service is from 5:30 to 6:00 and there is voluntary
samu until 7:30. There is a Sunday-afternoon session from 1:30
to 3:00.

Nagasakamachi, Kanazawa-shi, Ishikawa-ken 921. Tel: (0762)
41–2680. A twenty-minute bus ride from Kanazawa station.

大乗寺　石川県金沢市長坂町

SŌGENJI   This once-great Rinzai monastery in the countryside
of western Japan has recently been undergoing reconstruction
and is now offering Zen training to people at all levels. Many
foreigners have trained there. Currently three sesshin are scheduled
each month, two of five days each during which participants sit
for five hours every evening, and one of seven days in which they
sit all day. Outside these periods it is possible to live and train at
Sōgenji after consultations with the priest, who speaks some English. Life at the temple includes regular morning tai chi. A zazenkai is held at 8:00 A.M. every Sunday. Further information and
introductions can be obtained from the Institute for Zen Studies
in Kyoto.

1069 Maruyama, Okayama-shi, Okayama-ken 703. Tel: (0862) 77–8226. A thirty-minute bus ride from Okayama station.

曹源寺　岡山県岡山市円山 1069

ZENSHŌJI　This is a large Sōtō Zen temple in Hiroshima City. It offers occasional sesshin and a Friday zazenkai from 7:00 to 9:00 P.M., sometimes attended by foreigners.

556–115 Hesakachō, Higashi-ku, Hiroshima-shi, Hiroshima-ken 730. Tel: (0822) 29–0618. Near Hesaka station.

禅昌寺　広島県広島市東区戸坂町 556–115

CHŌSHŌJI　Chōshōji, a Sōtō Zen temple, is perhaps better known in places like India and California than in Japan. It is the family temple of priest Ryūhō Yamada, who lived in the United States for eight years and has an American wife. There is no schedule or program there, but foreign visitors are always welcome. "We're a receiving station for all kinds of people," says Shirley Yamada. "We want to service people with experience in mind expansion. We're not interested simply in Sōtō training so much as in a bigger spiritual movement. We try to give people the chance to realize their own enlightenment. We keep ourselves fluid to situations. We'll keep the lights on until 2:00 A.M. if people want to talk."

Many people who have undergone various kinds of spiritual training throughout the East, as well as in America and Europe, have picked up word on the grapevine that Chōshōji is a congenial place, and the Yamadas receive a lot of visitors. As mentioned, there is no formalized training, but it is possible to do zazen, and they have much experience in directing visitors to other temples. There are limited accommodation facilities. Chōshōji is in Beppu, one of Japan's most famous hot spring resorts, on the east coast of Kyushu. Many travelers to Kyushu pass through the city when they take the Osaka-Beppu ferry, one of the cheapest ways of reaching the island.

1–12–4 Asami, Beppu-shi, Ōita-ken 874. Tel: (0977) 22–4532. A ten-minute taxi ride from central Beppu.

長松寺　大分県別府市朝見 1–12–4

MYŌKŌJI　This Sōtō temple in Fukuoka City offers a thriving program for those who wish to practice Zen. A zazenkai is held every Saturday evening for two hours from 7:00. A zazenkai for children is held on Sunday morning from 7:00. A three-day sesshin is scheduled every month, and by consultation you can arrange further study and practice.

3–8–52 Yoshizuka, Hakata-ku, Fukuoka-shi, Fukuoka-ken 812. Tel: (092) 621–2698. A twenty-minute walk from Hakata station.

明光寺　福岡県福岡市博多区吉塚 3–8–52

JŌKOKUJI　Jōkokuji is a small Sōtō temple on the outskirts of Kumamoto City, offering a zazenkai every Wednesday evening from 8:00. Everyone is welcome. It is popular with local university students.

488 Takahira, Shimizumachi, Kumamoto-shi, Kumamoto-ken 860. Tel: (0963) 44–7603. A thirty-minute bus ride from Kumamoto station.

浄国寺　熊本県熊本市清水町高平 488

DAIJŌJI　Foreigners have trained at this Rinzai temple in Shikoku, and the Head Priest, Shindō Sawai, welcomes beginners and other visitors interested in Buddhism. Training is strict with an emphasis on natural food and plain living.

Tachima, Yoshidachō, Kita Uwa-gun, Ehime-ken 799–37. Tel: (08955) 2–1053.

大乗寺　愛媛県北宇和郡吉田町立間

Full-Time Training and Ordination

As mentioned in the Introduction, "conversion" to Buddhism is not a prerequisite for joining training sessions open to the public. However, one who wishes to do so may take lay ordination, called *zaike jukai* or *zaike tokudo*. There are no special conditions or requirements for this type of ordination other than sincere intent to follow the Buddhist way. Traditionally, one requests to receive the lay precepts from a priest with whom one has a special affinity. (Japanese parishioners often take lay ordination en masse from the high patriarch of their sect.) In a simple ceremony one takes the ten Mahayana precepts, promises to revere the Three Treasures (Buddha, Dharma, and Sangha), and vows to work for the salvation of all sentient beings.

In the old days monastic ordination, *shukke tokudo,* was a rather serious affair. One was, in principle, renouncing sex, property, and social ties. After Buddhism fell on hard times during the Meiji era (1868–1912)—there was no outright suppression but anti-Buddhist sentiment was strong and temples lost all public and much private support—Buddhist leaders felt that the only solution was to allow priests to marry, thus enabling them conveniently to reproduce disciples, rather than assiduously cultivate them. Nowadays, except in the case of nuns, there is no practical difference between lay and priestly ordination—priests can marry or remarry—and monastic ordination merely signifies the intention to receive formal training as a priest in a certain sect. The vows of monastic ordination are essentially the same as those of lay ordination: the monastic ordination ceremony is more elaborate, however, involving shaving of the head, reception of various robes and utensils, and other rites. In order to receive monastic ordination one must establish a solid relationship with, and obtain the assent of, a senior priest. The ordaining priest is one's *shisō,* "personal master." It is important to note that, unlike Christian ordination, Buddhist ordination marks the *beginning,* not the end, of one's training. In order to qualify as a full-time priest in charge of a temple (jūshoku) there are a variety of requirements that vary according to the sect. Since just about anyone may receive monastic ordination and eventually become a full priest (not a few temple sons are in fact forced to do so), foreign ordainees should be warned not to ascribe great cosmological significance to their ordination and a piece of paper certifying them as a "Teacher of the Law."

Upon monastic ordination one is theoretically committed to train in the honzan, the head temple of one's sect. (There are exceptions to this and certain Japanese priests train their foreign ordainees by themselves.) In principle, any male, regardless of nationality, who has been formally ordained and recommended by a member priest in good standing (including priests residing overseas) will be admitted to the head temple. One may be married when admitted to the head temple, but cannot, of course, live with one's wife during training in the monastery. The minimum stay used to be, and still is in a few places, three years. These days due to the shortage of priests many sects have reduced that period to a year, and university graduate students often only put in a few months.

Unfortunately the majority of monks at the head temple—mostly the sons of temple priests who will inherit the family business—are being detained unwillingly and cannot wait to escape so the atmosphere is hardly conducive to real practice. Further, monastery officials, mindful that this is their one chance to mold recalcitrant trainees, unmercifully haze their charges, occasionally with tragic results. Hard training is necessary, but sadistic discipline for mere discipline's sake is counterproductive. Foreigners have trained at most of the head temples, and all have survived the harsh conditions, stronger no doubt for the experience but not necessarily wiser. (The situation for Buddhist nuns is rather different. There is only a handful of ordained nuns here and they come from varied backgrounds. The main convent is the Aichi Semmon Nisōdō.)

The Kyoto Rinzai head temples and the two Sōtō head temples, Sōjiji and Eiheiji, are described elsewhere in this book. Eiheiji, it should be noted, fancies itself as the "Number One Dōjō in Japan," and if size and number of inmates are the criteria, it probably is. Now a huge complex, it is not at all like the small temple Dōgen founded in the thirteenth century. Proud of the monastery's strict image—although it is apparently not so strict: a monk was recently arrested there for growing and using marijuana—and conscious of what they perceive to be their superior calling, a lot of the monks go out of their way to act aloof and condescending. One experienced foreign trainee said of Eiheiji: "Altogether a rather unpleasant place; certainly not somewhere to visit to deepen your understanding of Zen." More promising are the *semmon dōjō* for ordained practitioners, listed below; most also allow lay participation and offer a good balance of strictness and correctness with proper spirit and understanding. However, these places are only for firmly committed practitioners with some experience; it is not possible to assume residence at any of them without an acceptable introduction or a trial period.

What happens when one "completes" one's training? If one has trained at the head temple and met the other requirements, the administrative headquarters (*shūmuchō*) issues a kind of diploma. Even though it is possible for a non-Japanese to head a temple in

Japan, most ordainees opt for returning home, to "beat the drum of the Dharma" in their native land.

ZUIGAKUIN   This temple located deep in the mountains of Yamanashi Prefecture was once the best place for serious Westerners to practice Zen. Unfortunately, the English-speaking monk formerly in charge accepted an assignment in the United States, and his replacement, a married priest with his own temple in another district, speaks no foreign languages. Foreigners will probably still be welcome to join the training, but it remains to be seen what direction this center will take.

Dai Bosatsu San Zuigakuin, Shimohatsukari, Hatsukarimachi, Ōtsuki-shi, Yamanashi-ken 409–11. There is no telephone so this place must be contacted by mail. Be sure to include a stamped, self-addressed envelope.

瑞岳院　山梨県大月市初狩町下初狩

HOSSHINJI   Many of the foreigners who helped transmit Zen from Japan to the West trained at Hosshinji, and today this monastery near the Japan Sea still attracts many non-Japanese. Over twenty people currently train there, including eleven foreigners. In general, they prefer you arrange an introduction through your teacher or another priest, but this is not vital. However, it is important to write in advance if you wish to arrange to stay there. They say they turn away those who arrive without previous notice.

Training is strict, and the temple attracts the more serious and experienced Zen practitioner. Although it officially belongs to the Sōtō sect, it has a tradition of rigid koan study. The current chief abbot, Secchi Harada Rōshi, has declared his willingness to meet serious students of Zen and discuss their training with them. They are also welcome to stay for several days. Those who wish to join for training are asked first to attend several sesshin. These are held during the first week of April, May, June, October, November, and December, and anyone is welcome, though it is important to have had some experience of zazen. Many foreigners living in Kyoto and other parts of Kansai attend regularly.

"Due to cultural and other differences we do not allow immediate entrance for long periods of stay," notes a foreign priest living at the temple. "But if people's aspirations are suitable to Hosshinji and they wish to stay longer, then, after perhaps three or four sesshin, they can apply to spend a period of training with us." The training periods are from March 25 to July 15 and from September 25 to February 15. "The basic deciding factor in whether we accept people for training is whether they are able to live harmoniously with the others," says the priest. Women are welcome to the sesshin, but are unlikely to be accepted for training. A small fee is charged for both sesshin and training.

Fushiwara, Obama-shi, Fukui-ken 917. Tel: (07705) 2–0525. A fifteen-minute walk from Obama station.

発心寺　福井県小浜市伏原

BUKKOKUJI　　Bukkokuji is a small Sōtō temple in Obama on the Japan Sea coast, very near the better known Hosshinji. Foreigners are welcome here at any time for stays of any length, and some have remained up to one year. "We accept anyone whose heart is pure and whose purpose is serious," says a priest there. It is preferred that visitors have a basic knowledge of Japanese. The daily schedule is similar to that of other temples such as Eiheiji, although it includes twenty minutes of early-morning jogging. Week-long sesshin are held in April, May, June, October, November, and December. The training at Bukkokuji is strict, but it is a small temple, and the overall atmosphere is friendly and relaxed. There are generally a few foreigners there, as well as some English-speaking Japanese. It is highly recommended for those who want a period of serious, full-time training in a temple, but do not feel ready for the long-term commitment of a place like

Hosshinji or Antaiji. Some foreigners living in Kyoto go to Buk-kokuji for the sesshin.

38 Fushiwara, Obama-shi, Fukui-ken 917. Tel: (07705) 2–3504. A ten-minute walk from Obama station.

仏国寺　福井県小浜市伏原 38

HAKUHŌJI　　Hakuhōji, a Sōtō Zen temple under the direction of Head Priest Chigen Sakimura, is an excellent place for serious, full-time practice. There are a minimum of distractions, and the emphasis is on "just sitting"—there are at least six one-hour meditation sessions a day. All of the foreign men (women are not allowed) who have trained there so far have been lay practitioners. Trainees lead a spartan life in the zendō, but the fees are extremely low. Write in English or call in Japanese for permission to visit this temple.

1551 Shimoterao, Chigasaki-shi, Kanagawa-ken 253. Tel: (0467) 51–8189.

白峰寺　神奈川県茅ヶ崎市下寺尾 1551

ANTAIJI　　Antaiji is a Sōtō temple for the serious student who speaks Japanese well, has practiced Zen already, and is prepared to stay at least six months. It was originally located in Kyoto and was headed by Kōshō Uchiyama Rōshi, who has taken a particular interest in foreigners. In the 1960s many of the Western-ers who drifted to Kyoto for Zen experiences ended up at Antaiji. Uchiyama Rōshi attracted so many disciples that the temple later moved to a remote spot in the mountains of Hyōgo Prefecture.

The current abbot, Kōhō Watanabe, is from Aomori Prefecture in northern Japan and has had a lot of experience in farming. The temple is now trying to become self-sufficient in foodstuffs.

Life at Antaiji is physically demanding, with much hard work in the fields and a lot of meditation. The actual schedule changes a lot, depending on the season, but there can be two to eight hours daily of zazen. Also, there are two sesshin each month, from the first to the fifth and for three days in the middle of the month. About twenty people live there, including some foreigners.

There is no standard procedure for applying to join, but due to their efforts to achieve self-sufficiency the Antaiji group must strictly limit how many practitioners they accept. They simply cannot support a great number. If you practice Zen in the Kyoto area you will meet people connected with Antaiji, and may gain an introduction. New members may be asked to supply their own boots and work clothes.

Reaching Antaiji is difficult. A three-hour train ride from Kyoto takes visitors to the nearest town, Hamasaka, on the San'in line, but this is sixteen kilometers from the temple. A bus goes ten kilometers of the remaining distance, but then it is necessary to walk, including three kilometers uphill. A newcomer would have great difficulty finding the place unaided. In winter there is heavy snow, and skis and snowshoes become absolutely necessary. Between December and mid-February it is almost impossible to reach Antaiji.

Kutoyama, Hamasakachō, Mikata-gun, Hyōgo-ken 669–67. Tel: (07968) 5–0023.

安泰寺　兵庫県美方郡浜坂町久斗山

RYŪTAKUJI　　Ryūtakuji is in Mishima, an attractive city at the foot of Mount Fuji and on the Shinkansen bullet-train line between Tokyo and Kyoto. Mishima is best known as the gateway to the Izu Peninsula, an area full of hot springs very popular with Tokyo holiday-makers.

Like Hosshinji, Ryūtakuji has played an important role in helping to transmit Japanese Buddhism to the West. For many years Sōen Nakagawa Rōshi was the abbot, and two American Zen leaders—Robert Aitken of the Diamond Sangha in Hawaii and Eidō Shimano of Dai Bosatsu in New York—trained there, as have many other foreigners, some for periods of several years. The temple offers Rinzai Zen in the Hakuin tradition. Sesshin are held monthly, usually from the 17 to the 25, from March to July and October to January. They are also held from November 15 to 25 and from December 1 to 9. A small fee is charged. Rates for long stays are said to be negotiable.

This is a serious monastery and training is strict. Do not expect any English. On no account should you turn up unannounced. Contact them in advance if you wish to stay, preferably with an introduction.

Sawaji, Mishima-shi, Shizuoka-ken 411. Tel: (0559) 86–2206. A ten-minute bus ride from Mishima station.

竜沢寺　静岡県三島市沢地

AICHI SEMMON NISŌDŌ   This Zen convent, Shōbōji, is one of the few places where women can train full-time as Buddhist nuns. Lately it has assumed a decidedly international flavor and currently four American women are training there. A delegation of Catholic sisters recently spent two weeks sharing the lives of the Buddhist nuns. Entrance, however, is difficult. You must either be an ordainee recommended by your master or undergo a long trial period as a lay student. A lay applicant must demonstrate communicable Japanese and some familiarity with Buddhist practice. Fees for nuns run about 200,000 yen a year. The terms are from April to July, September to December, and January to mid-March.

The daily schedule is as follows:

4:00 A.M.	Rise	1:30–3:00	Samu
4:15–5:00	Zazen	3:00–3:30	Tea time
5:00–6:15	Morning service	3:30–4:00	Free time
6:15–7:45	Cleaning	4:00–4:30	Evening service
7:45–8:15	Breakfast	4:30–5:30	Free time
8:15–9:30	Free time	5:30–6:00	Dinner
9:30–12:00	Class (see below)	6:00–8:15	Cleaning, bath, etc.
12:00–12:30	Lunch	8:15–9:00	Zazen
12:30–1:30	Free time	9:00	Lights out

The classes from 9:30 to 12:00 vary from day to day:

Monday	surplice sewing
Tuesday	kimono sewing
Wednesday	*Shōbōgenzō* lecture
Thursday	*Denkōroku* lecture
Friday	ikebana, chanting practice
Saturday	reciting practice, calligraphy
Sunday	(9:00–4:00) public zazen meeting women preferred, but men admitted

1–80 Shiroyamachō, Chikusa-ku, Nagoya-shi, Aichi-ken 464. Tel: (052) 751–2671. Four kilometers from Nagoya station.
愛知専門尼僧堂　愛知県名古屋市千種区城山町 1–80

ZUIŌJI　This traditional, strictly run Sōtō Zen training monastery in Shikoku, the smallest of Japan's four main islands, has accepted foreign priests, but usually only after they have been ordained and trained extensively elsewhere. Among Japanese practitioners it has the reputation of being one of the few places that maintain the ancient standards of Zen Buddhism. Serious monks go there from Eiheiji and other temples for "advanced" training. It is necessary to have an introduction.

One of Zuiōji's priests is living in a Catholic monastery in West Germany, guiding the monks there in zazen. Through his introduction some European Catholic priests have spent time training at Zuiōji.

Yamanechō, Niihama-shi, Ehime-ken 792. Tel: (0897) 41–6563. A ten-minute taxi ride from Niihama station on the Yosan line.
瑞応寺　愛媛県新居浜市山根町

PART TWO

RELATED ACTIVITIES

Temple Accommodations

Japanese temples, like some churches and monasteries in other countries, have a long tradition of taking in overnight guests. In the past these people were generally connected with the temple— they included itinerant monks, journeying scholars, pilgrims, and holidaying members of affiliated temples. But since the war rising costs have forced many temples, especially those with few parishioners, to seek novel ways of raising funds to maintain their buildings, and with the popularization of mass travel a new trend has arisen. More and more temples are now opening their premises to members of the public regardless of religious affiliation. In Japanese these are normally referred to as shukubō.

Some of these temples are associated with the Japan Minshuku Association, a grouping of family inns. Over eighty shrines and temples are affiliated with the youth hostel movement, and are listed in the annual handbook (which is partly in English). Other Japanese guidebooks, unfortunately now out of print, have listed up to four hundred temples and shrines in every part of the country which offer accommodations.

In most cases they are cheaper than hotels and can offer the foreign visitor an exotic experience in large, ancient, wooden-beamed rooms, sometimes containing Buddhist antiques and overlooking a picturesque garden. At some temples the overnight guest is allowed to join the morning sutra and prayer service. In a few cases this is compulsory.

Nevertheless, temple accommodations are mainly for the adventurous. Some people will not find the spartan conditions to their liking. Often the guest rooms are antiquated and dirty, with few facilities. The bedrooms may be large, but you can find yourself separated from a group of noisy students in the next room by just a thin, unlocked, sliding paper door. If the temple is crowded you may be expected to share your room with strangers. Do not expect any security. There will probably be no locks on the doors, and no front desk at which to deposit valuables.

Everything will be Japanese style. This means guests may have to lay out their own futon mattress and quilt at night and fold them up again the next morning. The toilets will be Japanese style, and the bath, if it exists, a communal one, perhaps even shared with the priest's family. Do not expect a television set.

Most temples impose an evening curfew of about 9:00, and guests will probably be woken at around 7:00 A.M. or earlier. Some places do not allow smoking or alcohol. All meals will probably be vegetarian and certainly Japanese style.

Basically, you are expected to behave as if you are a guest in someone's home (no matter how much the fee). Do not expect anyone at the temple to speak or understand English, and if you are unable to make yourself understood in Japanese you may be refused admission.

Reservations should be made in advance, preferably by mail, but telephone reservations are usually accepted. You may not be welcomed if you turn up without a booking. The temples and shrines listed in the youth hostel handbook could be considered an exception to this rule, although even there most Japanese will book in advance. One good reason for not turning up unannounced is that most temples have certain days of the year when they close their doors to the public due to special religious observances. And some temples which are listed as accepting guests in fact take only women. Finally, do not expect all temples to be old and exotic. Some look little different from modern office blocks.

Accommodations for Dewa Sanzan in northern Japan and those for Mount Kōya in Wakayama Prefecture are discussed in those entries. It is possible to book some shukubō, mainly those on Mount Kōya, through offices of the Japan Travel Bureau. The Tourist Information Centers in Tokyo and Kyoto can give up up-to-date lists of temples where foreigners have stayed.

The following temples are recommended. Expect to pay ¥2,000–4,500 per night, sometimes with meals, usually without.

KANNONJI   This small Jōdo temple houses a number of trainee priests and doubles as a youth hostel, offering dormitory accommodation to visitors to Noboribetsu. Guests sleep separately from the priests, but those with initiative will find there is still the chance to socialize. The premises resemble a small office building, but there is a modest temple room inside where a morning service is held early each day.

Noboribetsu is one of Japan's best-known hot spring resorts and attracts numerous visitors who believe the water here particularly efficacious for a wide variety of physical complaints. The nearby Valley of Hell, full of gushing and steaming mud and water, is popular with tourists.

119 Noboribetsu Onsenchō, Noboribetsu-shi, Hokkaidō 059–05. Tel: (01438) 4–2359. The temple is located in the heart of the hot springs area.

観音寺　北海道登別市登別温泉町 119

SAIMYŌJI   The twentieth stop on the Bandō thirty-three Kannon pilgrimage (see p. 112), Saimyōji attracts many visitors despite its rural location and the lack of public transportation. It is three kilometers from Mashiko, one of Japan's most famous pottery towns. Shōji Hamada, perhaps Japan's greatest modern potter, lived in Mashiko, and the town became famous worldwide when the British potter Bernard Leach also went there to work. Thousands of tourists flock to Mashiko, especially on weekends, to buy from the more than one hundred pottery workshops there.

Saimyōji, a Shingon temple, was founded in the eighth century, according to legend. It boasts a beautiful three-layered pagoda, built in the sixteenth century and designated as an important cultural property. There are hiking tracks in the surrounding hills and woods, and this is an ideal place for a weekend trip for those living in Tokyo.

Six small rooms and one large one accommodate about fifty guests in rather spartan fashion. Reservations are vital.

Mashiko, Mashikomachi, Haga-gun, Tochigi-ken 321–42. Tel: (02857) 2–2957. A ten-minute taxi ride or fifty-minute walk from Mashiko station.

西明寺　栃木県芳賀郡益子町益子

KŌMYŌJI　This large seaside Jōdo temple offers the only shukubō on a regular basis in Kamakura and is very popular. Reservations well in advance are vital. It was founded in the thirteenth century and boasts several grand old wooden structures as well as a large pond which is a blaze of red in early summer when the lotuses are in bloom. Some of the best views in the city are available from the surrounding hills. If you stay at the temple you may be expected to take part in the early morning service, as well as do half an hour or so of cleaning after breakfast.

Komyoji serves delicious shōjin ryōri lunch courses to the public. Bookings for these are also necessary several weeks in advance. If you are staying at the temple a separate reservation will be needed for the shōjin ryōri.

6–17–19 Zaimokuza, Kamakura-shi, Kanagawa-ken 248. Tel: (0467) 22–0603. A ten-minute bus ride from Kamakura station.

光明寺　神奈川県鎌倉市材木座 6–17–19

SHUNJŌIN   A seventeenth-century Rinzai Zen temple in the
resort seaside town of Matsuzakichō on the Izu Peninsula, a
popular weekend spot for Tokyo residents. Despite the beauty
of the temple, accommodation is in a modern two-floor building,
a little like a hotel. Two meals are included in the fee, and as those
visiting seaside resorts expect to eat fish, dinner here is not strictly
vegetarian. There is no program of zazen, but it is possible to
arrange with the priest for early morning sitting. The main attraction of the place for many people is the town's hot spring, and the
temple is connected to this, so guests can take advantage of the
healing waters. Hiking is possible in the surrounding hills.

　Shunjōin Kaikan, Matsuzakichō, Kamo-gun, Shizuoka-ken
410–36. Tel: (05584) 2–0719. A one-hour bus ride from Shimoda
station.

　春城院　静岡県賀茂郡松崎町

KAICHŌJI   This 350-year-old Rinzai Zen temple in the popular
hot-springs region of Shimizu City is very popular with Tokyo
people. Guests can take advantage of the spa facilities at the temple. Another attraction is the large stone and sand garden, built
this century. From the relics unearthed in the temple precincts it is
thought that there have been similar gardens for many years. One
of the attractions is the delicious shōjin ryōri dishes prepared
by the priest, and many tourists who are not staying at Kaichōji
nevertheless make a special diversion to eat lunch there. Reservations are necessary, and the price is higher than at most of the other
shukubō in this section. Overnight guests can also order the
Buddhist vegetarian meals, but they are not cheap.

　Sugiyama, Shimizu-shi, Shizuoka-ken 424–01. Tel: (0543) 67–
1320. A thirty-minute bus ride from Shimizu station.

　海潮寺　静岡県清水市杉山

TENSHŌJI AND ZENKŌJI   Takayama, known as "Little Kyoto," is a small, beautiful city in the Hida Mountains, part of the Japan Alps, north of Nagoya. Several temples in the city accommodate overnight guests. One is Zennōji, already mentioned (p. 62), on the outskirts of the city in the picturesque Teramachi area, at the foot of the surrounding hills. About a dozen temples are grouped here, including Tenshōji, which doubles as Takayama's youth hostel. It is two doors from Zennōji and is clearly signposted.

Nearer the center of the city is Zenkōji. The Takayama City tourist office often directs there visitors who wish to stay in a temple. The priest, whose brother works for the Los Angeles Hilton Hotel, speaks a little English and welcomes foreigners.

Tenshōji, 83 Tenshōjimachi, Takayama-shi, Gifu-ken 506. Tel: (0577) 32–6345. A fifteen-minute walk from Takayama station. Zenkōji, 4–3 Temmanmachi, Takayama-shi, Gifu-ken 506. Tel: (0577) 32–3804. A ten-minute walk from Takayama station.

天照寺　岐阜県高山市天性寺町 83
善光寺　岐阜県高山市天満町 4–3

TSUBAKI GRAND SHRINE　This shrine operates a special two-day program for foreigners who wish to experience Shintō, the ancient Japanese religion (p.63). The premises also include a beautiful tea house and garden. Guests can be accommodated in either Western-style or tatami rooms, and may join the daily training, which includes a morning service and purification rituals (*misogi*) under a waterfall. The cost is reasonable and includes two exquisite meals.

Yamamotochō, Suzuka-shi, Mie-ken 519–03. Tel: (0593) 71–1515. Further information can be obtained in English from Mr. Shunkichi Inokuma in the shrine's International Division, Hikawa Annex Building No. 2, Room 307, 6–9–5 Akasaka, Minato-ku, Tokyo 107. Tel: (03) 583–6637.

椿大神社　三重県鈴鹿市山本町
椿大神社東京講本部　東京都港区赤坂 6–9–5 氷川アネックス2号館 307

MYŌSHINJI   This is the headquarters of the Myōshinji branch of the Rinzai sect (p. 35). Two of the subtemples, Daishin'in and Tōrin'in, take overnight guests. It should be noted that while foreigners are not refused at either, it is preferable that you speak Japanese or be accompanied by someone who does.

Daishin'in, which was founded over five hundred years ago, is a small group of old, rather rickety buildings. It boasts its own small garden of swirling white sand, moss, trees, and colored rocks said to depict a dragon about to fly to the heavens. This is a tranquil haven, with birds and insects flying about, and if you reserve early, your room may be one of those overlooking this spot. Daishin'in has basic facilities: it offers a room, bedding, a small breakfast, and little else. But you will feel unmistakably that you are in a temple, with the garden, creaking old wooden verandahs, some beautiful calligraphy on the bedroom walls, and Buddhist statues scattered throughout the buildings. At night the place takes on a ghostly aspect, with a few soft lights and the dark silhouettes of the temple structures. Gongs at 6:00 A.M. signal the start of the morning service. Attendance is optional.

The other subtemple which takes overnight guests is Tōrin'in, which is thought to have been founded some 450 years ago. When the present priest took over it consisted of a leaky old building, few parishioners, and little income. Like some other priests in the same position, he took out a bank loan and built a new wing with ten air-conditioned guest rooms.

The whole place is clean, comfortable, and efficiently organized, but has little of the feel of a temple. There is a small library of books on Kyoto and a souvenir stand. Eighty percent of the guests are young women, and these are obviously preferred. Each of the rooms is named after a large Kyoto Zen temple; "Learn the name of your room and be happy," advises the comprehensive list of rules provided in each room. Loudspeakers pipe music around the building and announce the meal times.

The main reason to stay there is the food. The priest has been trained as a cook of shōjin ryōri, and the meals are delicious. A typical dinner might include eight lacquer bowls of vegetables in miso sauce, spinach cooked with sesame seeds, clear soup, tempura, sesame tofu, rice, pickles, and tea, all cooked according to traditional Buddhist methods, and served at small individual lacquer tables.

64 Myōshinjichō, Hanazono, Ukyō-ku, Kyoto 616. Daishin'in, tel: (075) 461–5714; Tōrin'in, tel: (075) 463–1334. Near Hanazono station on the San'in line.

妙心寺　京都市右京区花園妙心寺町 64

MYŌKENJI　Myōkenji is one of a cluster of Nichiren temples in northern Kyoto's Teranouchi district. It is well organized for visitors, and has space for over one hundred, in several large rooms and many smaller ones. Do not be startled to find a party of fifty or more schoolboys sharing the premises with you. Foreigners have been among the recent guests, so the temple has installed a Western-style toilet and has translated its regulations into English. Expect to find a little English spoken. The temple consists of a group of attractive old wooden buildings with creaky corridors running in all directions. A number of friendly young Japanese priests are usually living there. A morning service is performed daily at 5:30 (6:00 in winter) and all guests are invited.

Shimmachi Nishi Iru, Teranouchi, Kamigyō-ku, Kyoto 602. Tel: (075) 414–0808. A fifteen-minute bus ride from Kyoto station.

妙顕寺　京都市上京区寺之内新町西入ル

MYŌRENJI　This small, attractive Nichiren temple in the north of Kyoto is highly recommended for both its warmth and atmosphere. It was founded in 1294 and consists of several large wooden buildings, some, including the sleeping quarters, dating back two hundred years. It also boasts a stone and sand garden which was built this century and which in most Japanese cities would probably be famous, but which in Kyoto does not rate even a mention in the guidebooks. The screen door paintings are rated an important cultural property. A few large rooms are available for guests on an ad hoc basis, but these are often full with groups connected with the temple. Do not be surprised if you cannot get a room. If there is space, and if there are no special temple ceremonies that day, you will be welcomed by the woman in charge of accommodation, Mrs. Chizuko Iida, who speaks a little English and is very friendly to foreign visitors. The fee is cheap, with breakfast included. There is no bath, but public facilities are available nearby.

Teranouchi Higashi Iru, Ōmiya, Kamigyō-ku, Kyoto 602. Tel: (075) 451–3527. A fifteen-minute bus ride from Kyoto station.

妙蓮寺　京都市上京区大宮寺ノ内東入ル

CHISHAKUIN KAIKAN　　Chishakuin temple is the headquarters temple of a Shingon subsect, and is excellently located opposite the Kyoto National Museum and the popular Sanjūsangendō hall. It is a large temple with a famous old garden and a set of painted sliding screens which is designated a national treasure. Near the front gate of the temple complex is a new building, Chishakuin Kaikan, designed to accommodate guests. It is mainly intended for the sect's followers, who come in large groups from around Japan for religious conferences or Kyoto sightseeing, but if there is space members of the public are also permitted to stay. The building is like a cheap hotel, with a reception desk, souvenir shop, and large dining hall. The bedrooms are large and comfortable, and include pay television. The food is unremarkable and the atmosphere is far removed from that of a temple. In addition, its location at a busy intersection means that traffic noises continue all night.

The main attraction for foreigners will be the 6:00 morning service, which all guests are expected to attend. Walking to the main hall in the early morning mist can be a magical experience, as dozens of priests in colorful robes also slowly converge on the building from all parts of the grounds. The service begins with a forty-minute spectacular of chanting, singing, incense, gongs, chimes, and bells. Guests sit on the tatami floor at the back, but at one point are asked to stand and place some incense powder in a pot. Then everyone walks to an older and smaller temple building where the service continues in semidarkness, with a red-robed priest at the front tending a roaring fire while the priests chant to the beat of a huge drum. At the end guests are taken on a tour of the premises and receive tea and biscuits.

Shichijō, Higashiyama, Higashiyama-ku, Kyoto 605. Tel: (075) 541–5363. A five-minute bus ride from Kyoto station.

知積院会館　京都市東山区東山七条

MISHIMA SHRINE　This small Shinto shrine in the Higashi-yama area of Kyoto opened what it calls an "Economy Inn" on the premises in 1984, and offers nine Japanese-style rooms at very reasonable rates. All rooms include bathroom, toilet, air condi-tioner, heater, and television (the latter three cost extra). An English-language pamphlet is available at the Kyoto Tourist Information Center, and foreign visitors are encouraged, although little English is spoken.

As an inducement, male guests are invited to try on the robes of a Shinto priest, including wooden shoes, while women can dress as a shrine maiden and pose for a photograph. The real priest of the shrine says he is also hoping to introduce a pottery-making corner in the inn.

Mishima is thought to have been built in the twelfth century, and the enshrined deities are believed to help barren women to become pregnant, and pregnant women to give birth safely. One of the enshrined deities is said to be an eel, and on May 26 and October 26 each year local eel merchants and restaurant owners gather for the "Freeing the Eels" festival, at which they pray for the souls of the eels.

The shrine is most conveniently located, within walking distance of many of the sights of eastern Kyoto, including the Kiyomizu temple, the Sanjūsangendō hall, and the National Museum.

Kamiumachō, 3-chome, Higashiōji Higashi Iru, Shibutani-dōri, Higashiyama-ku, Kyoto 605. Tel: (075) 551–0033. A ten-minute bus ride from Kyoto station.

三島神社　京都市東山区渋谷通東大路東入ル三丁目上馬町

HIDEN'IN   This is a subtemple of Kyoto's Sen'yūji temple, a well-known sightseeing spot which is marked on most tourist maps. It offers warm, homely accommodation, and the Kyoto Tourist Information Center regularly directs there visitors who express a desire to stay in a temple. Foreigners are most welcome. The priest and his family compensate for their limited English with extreme friendliness. (This extended once to babysitting for an American couple who were staying with their baby and wished to experience the nightlife of Kyoto.)

Located on a hill, Hiden'in commands a beautiful view of Kyoto. It is a pretty temple, with an attractive orange front gate and several small gardens, including one in the middle of the main building. The guest rooms are new, and though they have little of the atmosphere of a temple they are clean and fresh.

Sen'yūji (Temple of the Bubbling Spring) is a central temple of the Shingon sect, and was founded in the thirteenth century. It took its name from a spring of fresh water which suddenly bubbled forth within the compound. Although close to the center of Kyoto it spreads over fifty-seven acres among hills and forests. For six centuries it was the mortuary of the Japanese Imperial family, and the tombs of many emperors are on the grounds.

35 Yamanouchichō, Sen'yūji, Higashiyama-ku, Kyoto 605. Tel: (075) 561–8781. A ten-minute walk from Tōfukuji station.

悲田院　京都市東山区泉涌寺山内町 35

SHIN YAKUSHIJI   No one with an ounce of adventure in him

will want to stay anywhere else when visiting Nara. Although the facilities are a little primitive, the atmosphere is everything to be expected in a temple complex containing some of the oldest buildings in Japan. There are only two drawbacks—the first is the location: although it is famous and is marked on all tourist maps, it is hidden among back streets, a twenty-minute walk from Nara station. The second problem is that once people have discovered the temple they are reluctant to leave.

Shin Yakushiji was founded in 747, and the main hall, built under the distant influence of Greek architecture, still remains from the eighth century. In Japan, only buildings at nearby Hōryū-ji are thought to be older. "The other buildings are all new," relates one of the priests there, pointing to structures built in the Kamakura era (1192–1333). Most of the statues in the hall are designated as national treasures, and one of the most famous, a scowling warrior deity, is pictured on the Japanese five-hundred-yen postage stamp.

Guests sleep in rooms decorated with Buddhist calligraphy in the rickety main temple building, behind the old hall. These quarters give much of the atmosphere of a rambling, run-down villa beside the Mediterranean, with creaking wooden corridors twisting into a tiny courtyard. All that is needed is a fountain. Whenever someone slides open one of the doors the whole building shakes. The numerous windows and doors open onto views of the surrounding gardens.

Clearly this temple is not trim and neat like many others: it resembles the seedy estate of a bankrupt millionaire. But the priests appear to take the view that the place has survived twelve hundred years and so is probably good for more centuries to come.

Get up early and walk about the small gardens before they are open to the day-trippers. Everything is ostensiby laid out formally, but somehow it doesn't work. The paths are cracked with weeds sprouting through. Some paving stones are missing. Overgrown trees and bushes flourish. In hidden corners are small ponds, bright orange Shinto torii shrine gates, flowers, stone lanterns, Buddhist statues, and stones engraved with calligraphy.

The temple is popular with young Japanese travelers, so reservations are vital. You may be asked to report by 6:00 P.M., and as there are no restaurants in the area it is advisable to eat before arriving. A small breakfast is served.

Takabatakechō, Nara-shi, Nara-ken 630. Tel: (0742) 22–3736. A twenty-minute walk from Nara station.

新薬師寺　奈良県奈良市高畑町

TŌNAN'IN   This is part of the famous Kimpusenji temple complex in the Yoshino Alps in Nara Prefecture, once much visited by pilgrims, but today mainly attracting hikers. The hills there have some 100,000 cherry trees, which are a blaze of color in April, when a well-known cherry-blossom festival is held. Many of the religious buildings in the Yoshino region were founded well over one thousand years ago. The temple itself is designated a national treasure, and the main fifteenth-century structure is the second-largest wooden building in Japan. The famous Deva kings at the gate were carved in the twelfth or thirteenth centuries. Many other famous sacred buildings also dot these mountains.

Tōnan'in produces a glossy pamphlet to advertise its accommodation facilities, which are extremely comfortable and a little more expensive than accommodations at many other temples. The pamphlet says that pilgrims have been staying at the temple since the eleventh century. One famous guest is said to have been Bashō, Japan's renowned haiku poet.

Following ancient Japanese religious traditions, some of the holy areas in the Yoshino Alps are for men only. Tōnan'in offers summer accommodation at a lodge atop one of the mountains, but only men are allowed to climb there. The main accommodation facilities, however, are for everyone. Buddhist vegetarian meals are available by reservation.

Yoshinoyama, Yoshinochō, Yoshino-gun, Nara-ken 639–31.

Tel: (07463) 2–3005. A fifteen-minute bus ride from Yoshino Jingū station on the Kintetsu Yoshino line.

東南院　奈良県吉野郡吉野町吉野山

JŌFUKUJI　　An old Shingon temple in the center of Shikoku, the smallest of Japan's four main islands, Jōfukuji boasts a fine collection of Buddhist statues and a friendly English-speaking priest. It has been listed in some English guidebooks, and foreigners have stayed there, sometimes for periods of up to a few weeks. It doubles as a youth hostel.

Aō, Ōtoyochō, Nagaoka-gun, Kōchi-ken 789–01. Tel: (08877) 4–0301. A twenty-five minute walk from Toyonaga station.

定福寺　高知県長岡郡大豊町粟生

Food for Practice

Following six years of frightful austerities, Buddha realized enlightenment after partaking of a nutritious dish called *payasa,* a kind of rice pudding made from milk, rice, crystal sugar, and fragrant spices. While he himself gratefully received whatever was put into his bowl—beggars cannot be choosers—going so far as to hasten his death by eating contaminated food served to him by a well-meaning but poorly prepared lay believer, Buddha was concerned that his disciples retain their health through proper diet. Monks should not eat after noon and simple food was best; however, rich, nutritious food such as payasa, ghee, oil, molasses, meat, and fish could be taken as medicine if necessary. It appears that the daily fare of a monk in Buddha's time consisted of milk and rice in the morning, a substantial midday meal of rice and (meat) curry, and an evening repast of fruit juice, sugar water, or molasses. Later, in the Gupta period (A.D. 320–540), breakfast was more commonly rice gruel, and dinner included rice, buttermilk, fruit, and, interestingly, a good ration of mildly narcotic betel leaves and nuts to be chewed to "aid digestion."

Although Buddha expressly permitted meat eating under most conditions, Chinese Buddhists by and large became fanatic vegetarians and temple food there was entirely meatless. That tradition was carried to Japan where this style of cooking was further developed and called shōjin ryōri, food for practice.

In Japan, shōjin ryōri has had a major influence on the local diet and food preparation. Such everyday comestibles as miso, tofu, *umeboshi* (pickled plums), and takuan pickles have their origin in Buddhist vegetarian cuisine, and the arrangement and display of classical Japanese cuisine is deeply rooted in Zen principles. Tea, both the beverage itself and the ceremony for drinking it, was promoted by Buddhist monks.

In the thirteenth century Dōgen laid down many of the rules to be followed by temples in preparing vegetarian fare, and these are still obeyed today. For instance, he insisted that all food be chosen first according to the season. It should be fresh, light, soft, clean, and not greasy. Every meal should be balanced with five flavors—soy sauce, salt, sugar, vinegar, and something hot or spicy; by five colors—red, yellow, green, black, and white; and food should be served according to five methods—raw, boiled, fried, steamed, and broiled.

The cooks should prepare even the smallest dish with complete concentration and sincerity. They should not discriminate between cheap and expensive ingredients, and, in fact, it is important to consider ways to cook common and cheap foods deliciously. The cooks must not waste ingredients, as these are part of the universe and are the gifts of nature. Even a drop of water should not be thrown away. Anything left over must be incorporated into soups or other dishes. The bowls and other containers should be carefully selected to be appropriate to the food. Dōgen also stressed that in the kitchen the cooks should not chat unnecessarily, and should at all times keep in mind the people who will eat the food.

Many temples or lineages of temples have their own vegetarian recipes which have been passed down through the centuries, and numerous collections of these have been published in Japanese. There are even a couple in English. Here are some typical examples of traditional Japanese vegetarian recipes: slivered mountain yam in horseradish and vinegar, turnip strips with sesame and mustard, lotus root with pickled plum sauce, spinach with tofu and sesame seed dressing, persimmons with peanut dressing, toasted walnuts, fried *shiitake* mushroom with tofu, sweet potato stew, winter melon and eggplant, candied chestnuts, mountain yam soup, rice with green peas, sesame seed tofu, and broiled zucchini with miso sauce. Such dishes are nowadays mainly served to honored guests only, or at special ceremonies. Trainees living in a monastery will generally receive meager servings of *okayu* gruel (rice mixed with barley) soup, pickles, and occasionally some vegetables.

Some temples supplement their incomes by serving Buddhist vegetarian courses to the public, and there are also a number of restaurants around the country which specialize in these dishes as well. Eating at one of these places is an excellent way for you to experience the traditional Buddhist cooking of Japan. (They are commercial operations, and no special rituals are involved. But special table manners are needed for temple training sessions. Everyone is assigned (or owns) a set of five *oryoki* bowls which fit neatly inside one another and are wrapped in a large napkin together with one's chopsticks and placed on a designated shelf. The proper procedure for using the bowls must be explained to newcomers since the ritual is complex and differs for each place. It takes some time to get accustomed to the correct method of arranging and putting away the bowls in conjunction with the accompanying chants, but once mastered one appreciates the efficiency and grace of the ceremony. Certain places such as Eiheiji, however, take excessive pride in their extraordinarily complicated dinner rite and the whole exercise irritates rather than elevates— a prime example of the unfortunate belief that if a little ritual is good, a lot must be better. Also, the expensive bowls required at Eiheiji would bankrupt a true mendicant.)

In Japan today shōjin ryōri is generally taken to mean vegetarian food. It is interesting to note that while Japanese shōjin ryōri restaurants present dishes cooked as naturally as possible, Chinese vegetarian restaurants often take incredible pains to make vegetables appear and taste like meat. Thus, one orders dishes of "Peking duck" and "sweet-and-sour pork" that are really cleverly disguised vegetables, tofu, and miso.

What can you expect at a shōjin ryōri restaurant? First of all, prices are generally very high and quantities small. Count on paying ¥2,500 per person at the cheapest place, and over ¥10,000 at some others. Reservations are normally required, and you should not be on a tight schedule—the esthetic and gustatory pleasures of a Buddhist vegetarian meal should be savored slowly. It is unlikely that any English will be spoken or understood, and the menu, where there is one, may be written in a cursive Japanese handwriting that even many Japanese people have trouble deciphering. At many places a minimum party of two to four is required.

It is no secret that many Buddhists prefer to take their rice in liquid form; sakè is a patent medicine for a variety of ailments. While no monastery is directly involved with rice wine production, a brewery in northern Japan markets one of its products under the label "Zen." There are thousands of brands of sakè in Japan, and many make an excellent accompaniment to a vegetarian feast. By coincidence, much of the finest sakè is made in the Kyoto region, one of the best being Tsuki-no-katsura. Other fine brands come from the chilly northern regions, like Dewazakura and Sumiyoshi from Yamagata, Urakasumi from Miyagi, and Shimeharitsuru and Hakkaisan from Niigata.

The following is a representative selection of temples and restaurants serving Buddhist vegetarian cuisine. There are many more, especially in Kyoto. The Tourist Information Centers in Tokyo and Kyoto can give up-to-date lists of places where foreigners have been welcomed.

MISHŌAN   This restaurant is in the Grand Hotel, which is part of the Sōtō Zen sect's headquarters building near central Tokyo. Although most of the hotel's rooms and facilities are Western style, the Mishōan restaurant on the fifth floor is purely Japanese, serving delicious shōjin ryōri courses. The atmosphere in the restaurant is more like that of a hotel than of a temple, but a big advantage is that there are sometimes English-speaking staff on duty to assist you, a rarity at a shōjin ryōri restaurant. In addition, the hotel has prepared various pamphlets in English, some of which give a little background information on shōjin ryōri and on some of the dishes served at Mishōan. Prices are high. Reservations at least one day in advance are necessary.

2–5–3 Shiba, Minato-ku, Tokyo 105. Tel: (03) 454–0311. A short walk from Shiba Kōen station on the Toei Mita subway line.

微笑庵　東京都港区芝 2-5-3

BODAIJU   The modest interior of this small new shōjin ryōri restaurant in Tokyo is hardly matched by the ambitions of the management, written in bold letters in English on one of the walls: "Bodaiju is the first vegetarian restaurant to introduce Chinese vegetarian dishes to Japan, and it is trying to encourage its good flavor with a view to eventually spreading the incomparable taste to every corner of the world. . . . It will be a great honor and pleasure if Bodaiju will contribute happiness and peace to mankind."

Few restaurant proprietors would cite "happiness and peace to mankind" as one of their goals, but the man who opened Bodaiju (Bodhi Tree—the sacred tree under which Buddha found enlightenment) is no ordinary restaurateur. He is Yehan Numata, the amazing entrepreneur behind the Buddhist Promoting Foundation, and Bodaiju, inside the Foundation's Tokyo headquarters building (p. 12), is just the latest of his diverse ventures aimed at spreading the word of Buddhism. If the way to a man's soul is through his stomach then Mr. Numata is a genius. The food at Bodaiju is superb.

Mr. Numata does not do things by halves. The chefs have been imported from Hong Kong, and they reckon to have a repertoire of some 350 dishes, based on recipes traditionally used in Chinese temples. Because of a lack of the necessary ingredients they are so far limited to offering just one hundred or so of their culinary masterpieces.

The food is quite unlike the delicately flavored dishes normally offered in Japanese temples. The flavors are full and spicy, as you would expect with Chinese cuisine. Also, as noted in the introduction to this chapter, much of the cooking attempts to use vegetables to imitate meat and fish dishes. Innumerable varieties of mushrooms, especially, taste remarkably like fish, and the cooks work wonders with various vegetables and tofu to create meatlike delicacies.

The extensive menu includes several courses which are the best value, though a minimum of two guests is necessary to order these. You can also order a la carte, but try and round up a large group to experience as great a variety as possible. Various potent Chinese liquors are also available. Prices are in the moderate to expensive range, but are a bargain for what you receive. This is one Chinese restaurant where you will not feel hungry again an hour later. Reservations are not vital, but are recommended. Also, try Bodaiju at lunchtime, when prices are cheap, and the place fills up with local office workers, who know a bargain when they see it.

Inside the Buddhist Promoting Foundation building at 4–3–14 Shiba, Minato-ku, Tokyo 108. Tel: (03) 456–3257. A short walk from Mita station on the Toei Mita subway line and Tamachi station on the Yamanote line.

菩薩樹　東京都港区芝 4–3–14 仏教伝道協会ビル

TONG FU　A fashionable Chinese restaurant and bar in Roppongi, one of the centers for expensive Tokyo nightlife, Tong Fu is a spacious place, with a courtyard, tropical plants, pop music, flashing lights, exotic Indian-style paintings, and young waiters with pencil moustaches and shiny black Chinese-style costumes. The food was described by one local English magazine as "nouveau Chinois," whatever that is. Among the dishes is one labeled as "monk's vegetarian set," modeled on traditional Chinese Buddhist recipes. It consists of soup with several tasty vegetable dishes, rice, dessert, and tea. It is moderately priced, and the dishes are changed each week.

6–7–11 Roppongi, Minato-ku, Tokyo 106. Tel: (03) 403–3527. A short walk from Roppongi station on the Hibiya subway line.

東風　東京都港区六本木 6-7-11

DAIGO　An elegant and very expensive shōjin ryōri restaurant convenient to central Tokyo. It was formerly known as Kakushō, because of its relationship with the famous Takayama restaurant of the same name. Among the dishes at Daigo are delicious sansai vegetables which are often hard to obtain in Tokyo. Reservations are vital at Daigo, and a minimum party of two guests is necessary.

2–4–2 Atago, Minato-ku, Tokyo 105. Tel: (03) 431–0811. A ten-minute walk from Kamiyachō station on the Hibiya subway line.

醍醐　東京都港区愛宕 2-4-2

SANKŌIN　In 1982 an English book on the shōjin ryōri of this Rinzai Zen nunnery in the western outskirts of Tokyo was published and since then the temple has become very popular with foreigners. An article on Sankōin's cuisine appeared in *Connoisseur* magazine and one of the nuns was invited to appear on American television with New York Times food critic Craig Clairborne.

Sankōin is only fifty years old, and is a small, pretty temple in a heavily built-up area. The recipes are centuries old, handed down from the mother temple in Kyoto. A meal at Sankōin is comparable to eating at a Kyoto temple, with the same delicately prepared vegetable and tofu dishes, the same attention to the natural tastes of the food, and the same gorgeous presentation.

Sankōin has been serving shōjin ryōri courses to the public for some twenty years, and is extremely popular. Reservations at least a month in advance are necessary. Prices have remained moderate, and this is probably the best deal in Tokyo for those who wish to try traditional Japanese temple cooking. There are two sittings each day, at midday and 2:00 P.M. It is closed on Thursdays and for some weeks in summer and winter. A minimum party of two is necessary.

3–1–36 Honchō, Koganei-shi, Tokyo 184. Tel: (0423) 81–1116. A ten-minute walk from Musashi Koganei station on the Chūō line.

三光院　東京都小金井市本町 3–1–36

KŌMYŌJI　This well-known Jōdo temple in Kamakura serves popular shōjin ryōri lunches in rooms normally off-limits to the public, overlooking the attractive garden. Reservations well in advance are vital, with a minimum party of two guests necessary. This is an excellent place for lunch while sightseeing in Kamakura. Prices are moderate. It is the only temple in Kamakura offering the public shōjin ryōri.

6–17–19 Zaimokuza, Kamakura-shi, Kanagawa-ken 248. Tel: (0467) 22–0603. A ten-minute bus ride from Kamakura station.

光明寺　神奈川県鎌倉市材木座 6–17–19

SAAMI　Saami is a small, quiet restaurant run by a friendly young couple on one of the shop-lined streets between Kamakura station and the famous Hachimangu shrine. It is a pleasant place to visit for lunch while sightseeing in the area. There is seating for about twenty-five in the wedge-shaped interior, which is decorated with thick bamboo stalks and attractive wooden and paper walls. A *bentō*—a lacquer lunchbox full of tempura, sesame tofu, boiled vegetables, soup, rice, and pickles—is reasonably priced, and full-course meals are also available.

1-6-4 Yukinoshita, Kamakura-shi, Kanagawa-ken 248. Tel: (0467) 25-0048. A five-minute walk from Kamakura station.

左阿弥　神奈川県鎌倉市雪ノ下 1-6-4

HACHIŌJI　　Hachiōji is a small, extremely beautiful Tendai temple set in a large bamboo grove in the hills of Saitama Prefecture, northwest of Tokyo. It is more commonly known as Takedera—the Bamboo Temple. Several hiking tracks pass nearby, and on weekends many walkers pause there to rest. But nowadays it is best known for its elaborate lunch, served daily in spring and autumn. These meals were first offered over twenty years ago, and today they are so popular—they are frequently featured in newspapers and magazines and on television—that it is usually necessary to reserve months in advance. Foreigners in Japan for just a short visit may find themselves able to take advantage of a cancellation, or their hotel may be able to obtain a booking for them at short notice.

One large temple room has been set aside for the meals, and about one hundred guests squeeze in, sitting in long lines on the tatami floor. You are expected to arrive by 11:30 A.M., and about twenty dishes will be served over two hours. Throughout the meal the priest acts as a cheerful emcee, handing around a microphone and calling on people to introduce themselves, cracking jokes, discussing the history of the temple, and conducting a running quiz in which you have to guess what you are eating (this is not at all easy). It is a little tiring, whether or not you understand Japanese, but the excellent meal makes up for it.

The food served depends on the season, but it is generally unlike shōjin ryōri at other temples. Most of the small dishes are vegetables, fruits, leaves, and flowers picked in the woods around the temple. For instance, you might receive one plate of tempura made

of different kinds of leaves, a small bowl of pine nuts, some cooked
dandelions, various parts of a pine tree, berries, mountain fruits,
and some sakè. It is all served in a table setting of leaves and
flowers, on bamboo bowls and plates. For chopsticks you must
manipulate two stalks of thin bamboo, which even the Japanese
find tricky. The price is moderate. After the meal the priest does a
roaring trade selling bamboo utensils.

704 Ōaza Minami, Hannō-shi, Saitama-ken 357. Tel: (04297)
7–0108. A thirty-minute taxi ride from Hannō station on the
Seibu Ikebukuro line or a thirty-minute bus ride and then a thirty-
minute walk.

八王寺　埼玉県飯能市大字南 704

KAKUSHŌ AND SHŌRENJI　　These are two excellent restaurants for visitors to Takayama, a picturesque city in the Japan
Alps. The popular restaurant Kakushō offers excellent shōjin ryōri
courses based on the sansai which make up much of the region's
cuisine. Many of these tasty vegetables will be quite unknown to
Westerners, and indeed many Japanese encounter some foods here
for the first time. Kakushō is open for lunch only, and a complete
course can take ninety minutes to serve. Customers sit on the
floor in their own room overlooking an attractive garden.

Kakushō is three hundred years old, and the present manager
is the eleventh-generation owner. The place has a very high reputation, not just in Takayama, but throughout Japan, and many
older Japanese make a point of eating a meal there when visiting
Takayama. Reservations are essential. Prices are high. The owner's
wife speaks some English.

Nearby, the Shōrenji temple serves shōjin ryōri meals between
11:00 A.M. and 6:00 P.M., at prices marginally less expensive than
those at Kakushō. This food, too, is based on mountain vegetables,
and some of the recipes date back over four hundred years. Shōrenji is also a popular temple for tourists, especially for its main

hall, built in 1504 and designated an important cultural property.

Kakushō is at 2–98 Babamachi, Takayama-shi, Gifu-ken 506. Tel: (0577) 32–0174. Shōrenji is at 8 Horibatamachi, Takayama-shi, Gifu-ken 506. Tel: (0577) 32–2052. Both are a fifteen-minute walk from Takayama station.

角正　岐阜県高山市馬場町 2–98
照蓮寺　岐阜県高山市堀端町 8

Izusen　Izusen is the name of a chain of shōjin ryōri restaurants based in Kyoto. With reasonable prices and attractive meals, often served in very pleasant surroundings, they are an excellent introduction to Buddhist vegetarian cooking. Go to the branch inside Daijiin, a subtemple of Daitokuji. There you sit outdoors on platforms among bushes and trees. It is quiet and surprisingly peaceful, despite up to one thousand visitors per day. Avoid the midday rush when busloads of visitors on package tours squeeze in. Also, in winter or rainy weather you will be jammed indoors, and when sitting outside in windy conditions you will likely be bombarded with leaves.

The reasonably priced "Miyako" (capital city) course offers you a generous trayful of a dozen bowls, with bitter green tea, a small Kyoto-style sweet, sesame tofu, tempura, many kinds of vegetables, soup, rice, and pickles. All are beautifully arranged. At the end of the meal seven of the bright red lacquer bowls fit neatly into one another.

Reservations are not needed, although in busy periods it is sometimes necessary to wait for a place, as it is very popular with tourists to Kyoto.

The Daitokuji branch is at 53 Daitokujichō, Murasakino, Kita-ku, Kyoto 603. Tel: (075) 491–6665. Another branch is right outside the main Daitokuji gate, at 42 Monzenchō, Murasakino, Kita-ku, Kyoto 603. Tel: (075) 493–0889. A third branch is in the second floor of the building next to the Tourist Information Center, at Shichijō Sagaru, Karasuma-dōri, Sakyō-ku, Kyoto 606. Tel: (075) 343–4211.

泉仙　京都市北区紫野大徳寺町 53
　　　京都市北区紫野門前町 42
　　　京都市左京区烏丸通七条下ル　駿河屋ビル内

IKKYŪ　Ikkyū has a reputation for serving some of the finest shōjin ryōri dishes in Kyoto. Naturally, it is also very expensive. For 450 years it has also been supplying food to Daitokuji temple, and is especially famous for its *nattō,* a pungent concoction of fermented soy beans. Everything is very formal, in the highest tradition of Kyoto restaurants. You will be received with a lot of bowing and escorted to your own tatami room. Waitresses in kimono will take your order and serve your food. Expect some tea and a sweet, followed by rice, vegetables, tofu, and miso soup containing the famous nattō. Everything is beautifully prepared. The actual food will depend on the season. All the tastes are light and subtle. The quantities are tiny.

If you are a connoisseur of fine Japanese food and are prepared to pay the price you will enjoy Ikkyū. Otherwise, you may prefer a place like Izusen, which has a branch just a few doors away. It serves larger meals at a fraction of Ikkyū's costs.

A minimum party of two is normally necessary to eat at Ikkyū, and reservations are vital.

20 Daitokuji Monzen, Murasakino, Kita-ku, Kyoto 603. Tel: (075) 493–0019. Right by the entrance to Daitokuji temple.

一久　京都市北区紫野大徳寺門前 20

IKKYŪAN　A pleasant, two-story restaurant in the heart of colorful eastern Kyoto, between Kiyomizu temple and the Heian shrine. It is an excellent spot for lunch while exploring that area. The tatami-floored rooms are bright and airy, and many have excellent views of the surrounding trees, temples, shrines, and pagoda.

Much of the food is cooked in tangy sauces and the tastes are stronger than at other shōjin ryōri restaurants, and perhaps more to the immediate liking of many foreigners. A typical meal might start with a cup of bitter green tea and a sesame-flavored sweet, followed by sesame tofu, some juicy pink tofu, glazed cherries, cucumber in sesame sauce, hot boiled vegetables in a sweet sauce, a plate of cold vegetables, tempura, egg plant in miso sauce, rice, clear soup, pickles, a slice of watermelon, and a pot of green tea. Quantities and prices are moderate. Reservations are necessary.

Kōdaiji Minamimon-mae, Higashiyama-ku, Kyoto 605. Tel: (075) 561–1901. Next to Kōdaiji temple, and a few minutes from Maruyama Park.

一休庵　京都市東山区高台寺南門前

NANZENJI　This is one of the great Rinzai monasteries. Over the years Nanzenji has become associated with *yudōfu,* a simple, but tasty and healthy dish of tofu and vegetables cooked in steaming water in a large bowl at your table. Two subtemples, Chōshōin and Kōan, serve this and moderately priced and popular shōjin ryōri courses. Chōshōin is a six-hundred-year-old building, and in fine weather customers can sit outdoors in a small but attractive garden. This is especially pleasant in autumn when the leaves turn a bright red. Kōan's food is equally delicious and a little more expensive. No reservations are necessary.

Fukuchichō, Nanzenji, Sakyō-ku, Kyoto 606. Chōshōin, tel: (075) 761–2186. Kōan, tel: (075) 771–2781.

南禅寺　京都市左京区南禅寺福地町

RYŌANJI　Ryōanji is most famous for its garden of rock and sand. Less well-known is its beautiful large lake, which attracts hundreds of ducks. On one of the shores is a lovely restaurant called Saigen'in, serving yudōfu and a shōjin ryōri lunch course at reasonable prices. It is best in warm weather when the sliding doors are opened and guests can eat while looking out over a small garden and the lake. Reservations are not needed.

Goryōnoshitachō, Ryōanji, Ukyō-ku, Kyoto 616. Tel: (075) 462–4742. A fifteen-minute walk from Ryōanji station on the Keifuku Electric Railway Kitano line. Marked on every tourist map.

竜安寺　京都市右京区竜安寺御陵ノ下町

TENRYŪJI　Visitors to this famous monastery can order tasty shōjin ryōri lunch courses which are served in private rooms overlooking the famous garden. This is not a restaurant, and the meals are served on something of an ad-hoc basis, at lunchtime only, and providing they have enough food. Prices are moderate. Phone first, or inquire at the ticket booth as soon as you arrive.

68, Susukinobabachō, Saga Tenryūji, Ukyō-ku, Kyoto 616. Tel: (075) 881–1235.

天竜寺　京都市右京区嵯峨天竜寺芒ノ馬場町 68

MAMPUKUJI AND HAKUUN'AN　Mampukuji, the head temple of the Ōbaku school of Zen, operates a restaurant serving delicious shōjin ryōri courses derived from Chinese recipes. This style of cooking, using more oil to cook the foods than in Japanese shōjin ryōri, originated at Mampukuji, and is usually called *fucha* (ordinary food) *ryōri*. The final taste is a little stronger than at most other Kyoto temples, but otherwise fucha cuisine is not greatly different. The food is served on large plates instead of the small, delicate bowls more common at such restaurants. A minimum party of four is necessary, and reservations are vital. Prices are moderate.

Across the road from Mampukuji's main entrance is Hakuun'an, which serves similar dishes at similar prices and will accept individual guests. It overlooks its own attractive garden with a lake and a bamboo grove. Reservations are recommended.

If you are sightseeing in the Uji area of Kyoto consider calling at one of these places for lunch.

The address for both places is Sambanwari, Gokanoshō, Uji-shi, Kyoto-fu 611. The telephone number of Mampukuji is (0774) 32–3900, and that of Hakuun'an is (0774) 31–8017. A five-minute walk from Ōbaku stations on the Japan National Railways Nara line and the Keihan Electric Railway Uji line.

万福寺・白雲庵　京都府宇治市五ヶ庄三番割

Pilgrimages

Pilgrimages are walking Zen; step by step the practitioner makes his or her way through blue sky temples and white cloud monasteries. Conducted in the traditional manner—on foot, in old-fashioned garb, carrying no money, accepting whatever comes—pilgrimages are among the most demanding, and therefore most rewarding, of all religious disciplines. Buddhist temple pilgrimages have a long history in Japan but may now be more popular than ever, attracting millions of people every year. Many foreigners have joined various treks, with a few, including several women, completing the famous two-month Shikoku pilgrimage in commemoration of the Shingon patriarch Kōbō Daishi. Most of the other pilgrimages in Japan are connected with Kannon, the Goddess of Mercy, who is regarded as a deity of the common people. "Kannon laughs with the people when they are happy, and cries with them when they are sad," says a Japanese saying, and Kannon worship is common to all the Buddhist sects. Many of Japan's most famous Buddhist statues are of Kannon, and the pilgrims travel to worship at these. Kannon is believed to be able to manifest herself in thirty-three forms and pilgrimages often consist of thirty-three temples in one region.

Traditionally, a pilgrim was dressed in white breeches and

jacket, straw sandals, and a straw hat, and walked the entire route carrying a staff. In Shikoku this staff represents Kōbō Daishi, as he travels with every pilgrim; on the Kannon pilgrimages, it represents the Goddess. The staff is a pilgrim's most important possession, and its tip and base—its face and feet—should be washed carefully at every overnight stop, even before one washes oneself.

Today, however, most pilgrims travel by bus or taxi, often on tours organized by local travel companies. They wear everyday clothes, with perhaps just a white scarf bearing the crest of the travel firm draped around their neck. On board their bus they relax with music and drink, and at the temples they sometimes play cassettes of the sutras, rather than chanting themselves.

There is something to be said for this twentieth-century approach. Some segments of the pilgrimage are rather long, and walking can be arduous in the Japanese summer and winter. In addition, many of the rural tracks have now disappeared, and you sometimes have no alternative but to walk for miles alongside a busy highway, dodging the traffic. Nevertheless, the true pilgrim will choose to walk the circuitous route on his or her own sturdy legs.

As a general rule, your fellow pilgrims will be older people, and you can expect twice as many women as men. Often they have recently suffered some loss, usually the death of a loved one. Others feel the need to expiate some wrongdoing. Many do the same pilgrimage numerous times, as often as once or twice a year. (One eighty-six-year-old pilgrim has made the Shikoku route forty-five times and is still at it.) Even traveling by bus can be a strain for these older people, as a lot of the temples still require a steep walk, sometimes up hundreds of steps.

It must be recognized that the person with just a scanty knowledge of Japanese will find it very difficult to attempt one of these pilgrimages alone. Maps and instructions are all but indispensable for locating many of the temples, which are often tucked away in remote country lanes, far from main traffic routes. But apart from a couple of general books about the Shikoku pilgrimage no practical information is available in English and would-be foreign pilgrims must rely on Japanese guidebooks. The most notable of these is the *Koji Junrei* (Pilgrimages to Ancient Temples) series published by the Manganji temple and its priest, Ryōyū Hirahata. (9822–1, Tennōdai Chōshi-shi, Chiba-ken. Tel: (0479) 24–8416.) This series covers nine pilgrimages throughout Japan. The books are generally not available in bookshops, but are usually on sale at many of the temples they cover. (If in Tokyo, one place where you can buy them is at the famous Asakusa Kannon temple, Sensōji) Other books are available for some of the more popular pilgrimages, and you may find these in the guidebook departments of large bookshops. The notes that follow are intended as no more than a brief introduction to some of the more popular pilgrimages.

Pilgrims should buy at their first stop a *nōkyōchō,* a folding book with blank pages, and at each temple ask for its *hanko* (seal) and inscription. At the end of your pilgrimage you will have a memorable record. A lot of the seals are centuries old, while the calligraphy of many priests is nothing less than art.

THE EIGHTY-EIGHT TEMPLES OF SHIKOKU   Shikoku is the smallest of Japan's four main islands, but the pilgrimage here of eighty-eight temples is the most famous in the country. It generally takes forty to sixty days to complete on foot, and you circle the entire island. Although the main inspiration is Kōbō Daishi, who was born on the island in 774, the pilgrimage attracts Buddhists of all sects. Its origin is not clear. Many people claim that Kōbō Daishi himself visited all the temples—and each claims some connection with him—but this is far from certain. For many centuries it was mainly a form of ascetic training for Shingon monks, and only over the past 150 years or so has it become popular with ordinary people. By tradition, you should call at Mount Kōya for a blessing before beginning the pilgrimage.

Westerners have completed and written about the Shikoku pilgrimage. The best book in English on the subject, and on pilgrimages in Japan in general, is *Japanese Pilgrimage* by Oliver Statler (C. E. Tuttle). Statler, the author of several memorable books on Japan, has walked the pilgrimage several times, and the book is a distillation of his experiences.

THE THIRTY-THREE TEMPLES OF SAIGOKU   This Kannon pilgrimage takes in some of the celebrated temples of Kyoto and the surrounding area in western Japan. (*Saigoku* means "west country.") Though there are only thirty-three temples, they are spread far apart, and it can take up to three months to cover them all on foot. Even by car it may take nearly two weeks.

As with virtually every other pilgrimage, its origins are lost in history; all that are left are many legends. One of these, very similar to the myths surrounding numerous other pilgrimages, is that a court noble in the eighth century took to visiting the thirty-three Kannon temples to expunge the grief resulting from the death of a lover.

The pilgrimage begins in Wakayama Prefecture, south of Kyoto, moves to the historic areas of Kyoto and Nara, and travels on to Osaka and several other regions before finishing many miles away in Gifu Prefecture. The route takes you through largely rural areas, yet the temples are often grand structures, quite unlike the little country temples of other pilgrimages. The most famous is probably Kiyomizu temple, a gorgeous wooden complex set in the hills of Kyoto and one of the city's most famous tourist attractions.

THE THIRTY-THREE TEMPLES OF MOGAMI RIVER   The Mogami River flows through the heart of Yamagata Prefecture in northern Japan, fertilizing the land and helping the local farmers produce some of the country's finest rice and fruits. The river is best known in Japan for Bashō's seventeenth-century verse, regarded by many as perhaps the finest of all his celebrated haiku:

> May rains,
> Gathering swiftly,
> Rushing into Mogami River.

Since the eighth century the river has been known for the concentration near its banks of temples possessing images of Kannon, attracting the devout, and a thirty-three-temple pilgrimage gradually evolved.

With one exception—Yamadera—all the temples are small family establishments, and this pilgrimage will take you to the heart of rural Japan. By contrast, Yamadera (also visited by Bashō, whose mind was "cleansed by the profound stillness of the area's ineffable beauty") is a large mountain temple complex of ancient wooden buildings scattered among huge rocks and soaring cedars; even though the buildings are now rather run-down and poorly maintained the scenery is magnificent and it remains one of the prime tourist sights of northern Japan.

THE THIRTY-THREE TEMPLES OF BANDŌ   This thirty-three-Kannon pilgrimage, with a history of several centuries, perhaps owes some of its popularity to its proximity to Tokyo, and its inclusion of the Asakusa Sensōji temple, undoubtedly the best-known temple in the capital city and often referred to simply as the Asakusa Kannon temple. It starts in Kamakura, an ancient capital of Japan, and takes in several of the well-known temples of that city. Many Tokyo people turn this pilgrimage into a weekend affair, traveling to one area on a Saturday or Sunday and "doing" all the temples there, regardless of the prescribed order. Apart from Tokyo and Kamakura this pilgrimage will take you to many quaint country temples in Saitama, Gumma, Tochigi, Ibaraki, and Chiba prefectures, all just a short distance from Tokyo.

THE THIRTY-FOUR TEMPLES OF CHICHIBU   The Chichibu thirty-four-Kannon-temple pilgrimage once attracted only the most devout to its tiny temples nestled in rugged mountains west of Tokyo. But today, with the rapid growth of the capital city and its transportation facilities, the temples are easily accessible, and this pilgrimage has become one of the most popular in the country. Every weekend thousands of day-trippers swarm to the Chichibu mountains for hiking, picnics, and sightseeing, and many combine this with a "pilgrimage" to the temples.

Again, the origin of the pilgrimage is not known, although it is thought there have been Kannon temples in these hills since at least the tenth century. It is a mystery why there should be thirty-four temples on the pilgrimage, instead of the traditional thirty-three. One theory is that it was to allow those who completed the Saigoku, Bandō, and Chichibu pilgrimages to boast that they had visited a round number of one hundred temples, instead of an inauspicious ninety-nine.

Buddhist Universities

Although most of these institutions were once primarily seminaries, Buddhist Studies is now only one of the many departments they contain. All are rather secularized, run in the same manner as any other private college. Foreigners have studied at most of the places listed here but the instruction is all in Japanese and there are no special provisions made for English-speaking students. A few have, or had, foreign instructors on their staff.

SŌTŌ ZEN

Komazawa University
1–23–1 Komazawa
Setagaya-ku, Tokyo 154
Tel: (03) 422–6111
駒沢大学　世田谷区駒沢 1–23–1

Aichi Gakuin University
Nisshinchō, Aichi-gun
Aichi-ken 470–01
Tel: (05617) 3–1111
愛知学院大学　愛知県愛知郡日進町

Tōhoku Social Welfare University
(Tōhoku Fukushi Daigaku)
1–8–1 Kunimi

Sendai-shi, Miyagi-ken 980
Tel: (0222) 33–3111
東北福祉大学　宮城県仙台市国見
　1–8–1

RINZAI ZEN

Hanazono University
8–1 Tsubonouchichō
Nishinokyō, Nakagyō-ku
Kyoto 604
Tel: (075) 811–5181
花園大学　京都市中京区西ノ京
　壹ノ内町 8–1

TRUE PURE LAND BUDDHISM
(Jōdo Shin)

Ryūkoku University
Tsukamotochō, Fukakusa
Fushimi-ku, Kyoto 612
Tel: (075) 641–7261
竜谷大学　京都市伏見区深草塚本町

Ōtani University
22 Kamifusachō
Koyama, Kita-ku
Kyoto 603
Tel: (075) 432–3131
大谷大学　京都市北区小山上総町 22

PURE LAND BUDDHISM (Jōdo)

Bukkyō University
96 Kita Hananobōchō
Murasakino, Kita-ku
Kyoto 603
Tel: (075) 491–2141
仏教大学　京都市北区紫野
　北花ノ坊町 96

SHINGON BUDDHISM

Kōyasan University
385 Kōyasan, Kōyamachi,
Ito-gun, Wakayama-ken 648
Tel: (07365) 6–2921
高野山大学　和歌山県伊都郡高野町
　高野山 385

Shuchiin University
545 Tōjichō, Hachijō Sagaru
Mibu-dōri, Minami-ku
Kyoto 601
Tel: (075) 681–6513
種智院大学　京都市南区壬生通八条
　下ル東寺町 545

Taishō University
3–20–1 Nishi Sugamo
Toshima-ku, Tokyo 170
Tel: (03) 918–7311
大正大学　豊島区西巣鴨 3–20–1

(Taishō University is jointly
sponsored by Jōdo, Tendai,
and two Shingon sects.)

NICHIREN BUDDHISM

Risshō University
4–2–16 Ōsaki
Shinagawa-ku, Tokyo 141
Tel: (03) 492–6611
立正大学　品川区大崎 4–2–16

Japan Social Welfare University
(Nihon Fukushi Daigaku)
31 Takikawachō, Shōwa-ku
Nagoya-shi, Aichi-ken 466
Tel: (052) 833–8173
日本福祉大学　愛知県名古屋市
　昭和区滝川町 31

Most of the public universities maintain a small Buddhist
Studies department; foreigners have studied at Tokyo,
Kyoto, and Tōhoku Universities.

Recommended Reading

The following books offer a general introduction to
Buddhism from several different points of view:

Conze, Edward. *Buddhism: Its Essence and Development*. New York:
Harper and Row, 1959.

Kalupahana, David J., and Indrani Kalupahana. *The Way of Siddhartha*.
Boulder: Shambhala, 1982.

Mizuno, Kogen. *The Beginnings of Buddhism*. Tokyo: Kōsei Publishing
Co., 1980.

Nakamura, Hajime. *Gotama Buddha*. Tokyo: Buddhist Books International, 1977. Available from Eikyōji Institute of Buddhist Studies.

Rahula, Walpole. *What the Buddha Taught*. New York, Grove Press,
1962.

Due to the practical orientation of this book, we did
not include information on the historical background
of Japanese Buddhism or provide details on the
various sects. That information is readily available
in two inexpensive paperback books:

Arai, Ken et al. *Japanese Religion*. Tokyo: Kodansha International,

1981. This book covers all aspects of Japanese religion. It gives brief descriptions of all the Japanese Buddhist sects, including addresses and telephone numbers of their respective headquarters.

Saunders, Dale E. *Buddhism in Japan*. Tokyo: C.E. Tuttle, 1972. A historical study of Japanese Buddhism.

For more detailed information, see the following two books. They are available in many libraries and some second-hand bookstores.

Eliot, Sir Charles. *Japanese Buddhism*. London: Routledge and Kegan Paul, 1964.

Takakusu, Junjiro. *The Essentials of Buddhist Philosophy*. Honolulu: East West Center, 1956.

There are many introductions to Zen Buddhism, but the following two books are classics, and deserve to be read by everyone interested in the subject:

Suzuki, D.T. *Zen and Japanese Culture*. Princeton: Bollingen, 1973.

Suzuki, Shunryu. *Zen Mind, Beginner's Mind*. Tokyo: John Weatherhill, 1970.

Two illustrated accounts of life in a traditional Zen monastery have been published:

Satō, Giei. *Unsui: A Diary of Zen Monastic Life*. Honolulu: University Press of Hawaii, 1973. This book is available in Japan through the Institute for Zen Studies.

Satō, Kōji. *The Zen Life*. Tokyo: John Weatherhill, 1972.

Two interpretations of the practice of zazen are presented in the following books:

Sekida, Katsuki. *Zen Training*. Tokyo: John Weatherhill, 1975.

Uchiyama, Kōshō. *Approach to Zen*. Tokyo: Japan Publications, 1973.

General travel guidebooks can also be very helpful, providing information on temples and their history as well as assisting those planning pilgrimages.

Brown, Jan. *Exploring Tohoku*. Tokyo: John Weatherhill, 1982.

Cooper, Michael. *Exploring Kamakura*. Tokyo: John Weatherhill, 1982.

Japan Travel Bureau. *Travel Guide Japan*. Tokyo: Japan Travel Bureau, 1983.

Mosher, Gouverneur. *Kyoto: A Contemplative Guide*. Tokyo: C.E. Tuttle, 1978.

Plutschow, Herbert E. *Historical Kyoto*. Tokyo: Japan Times, 1983.

———. *Historical Nara*. Tokyo: Japan Times, 1983.

Finding List

The "weathermark" identifies this book as a production of John Weatherhill, Inc., publishers of fine books on Asia and the Pacific. Editorial supervision: Jeffrey R. Hunter. Book design and typography: Miriam F. Yamaguchi. Production supervisor: Mitsuo Okado. Composition of text: Korea Textbook Co., Seoul. Printing: Shōbundō Printing Co., Tokyo. Binding: Makoto Binding Co., Tokyo. The typeface used is Monotype Times New Roman.

ABOUT THE AUTHORS

MARTIN ROTH, a native New Zealander, is a long-time Tokyo resident. As an international journalist, he has covered Asia for newspapers and magazines around the world. An avid trekker to Zen monasteries, he now works for a securities firm in Tokyo.

JOHN STEVENS is a well-known Buddhist scholar and Zen monk. Born in the United States, he now resides in Sendai, Japan and is the author and translator of several books on the martial arts, Zen art, and Zen poetry, including *One Robe, One Bowl* and *Mountain Tasting*.